The Estate Planning Sourcebook

Also by Dawn Bradley Berry:

The Divorce Recovery Sourcebook

The Divorce Sourcebook

The Domestic Violence Sourcebook

The 50 Most Influential Women in American Law

Equal Compensation for Women

The Estate Planning Sourcebook

Dawn Bradley Berry

LOWELL HOUSE
LOS ANGELES
NTC/Contemporary Publishing Group

Library of Congress Cataloging-in-Publication Data

Berry, Dawn Bradley.
The estate planning sourcebook / by Dawn Bradley Berry.
p. cm.
Includes bibliographical references and index.
ISBN 0-7373-0076-0
1. Estate planning–United States–Popular works. I. Title.
KF750.Z9B475 1999
346.7305'2–dc21 99-17385
CIP

Published by Lowell House
A division of NTC/Contemporary Publishing Group, Inc.
4255 West Touhy Avenue, Lincolnwood (Chicago), Illinois 60646-1975 U.S.A.

Printed in the United States of America
International Standard Book Number: 0-7373-0076-0
99 00 01 02 03 04 RRD 18 17 16 15 14 13 12 11 10 9 8 7 6 5 4 3 2 1

Design by S. Pomeroy

CONTENTS

Caveat

This book is intended as a guideline to help readers acquire general information about the various aspects of estate planning. I hope it will help you to feel more knowledgeable and better able to frame your questions when you seek the assistance of an attorney and other professionals in formulating your estate plan. The information provided here is not intended as legal advice, nor is it meant to replace individualized professional assistance. My goal is to help you work with these people to be sure that your estate plan achieves your objectives, that it is created as efficiently and inexpensively as possible, and that it is done, above all, right.

This book is also not a do-it-yourself manual to help you prepare your own estate planning documents without the help of professional advisers. Because each person's legal needs vary, and because the laws and regulations of each state are different and constantly changing, I have not included any forms or fill-in-the blank documents. In fact, one of my primary goals in writing this book is to strongly discourage anyone—no matter how "simple" his estate may appear—from trying to prepare the legal documents required for an estate plan without qualified professional assistance.

Many other books purport to give you everything you need to do it all yourself. Some contain valuable information, some are even listed in my recommended reading list at the end of this book. But I urge you to use this book and any others you consult to arm yourself with the knowledge to work *in partnership* with attorneys, financial planners, accountants, and insurance agents—and to disregard anyone or anything that purports to replace the customized, individual help provided by qualified professionals who can tailor their recommendations to meet your unique needs and circumstances.

Equally significant is my goal to emphasize the importance of understanding what the various components of estate planning are intended to accomplish, as well as what the documents mean and how they work together. Approaching a professional with your documents organized, your questions framed, and a storehouse of basic knowledge and intelligent ideas can give you a head start and save you time and money. Perhaps even more importantly, once you understand the basic goals and components of estate planning, you will never feel the need to place blind trust in the assurances of an attorney or other professional.

Of course, you should choose advisers you feel are competent and trustworthy, but you should also insist that each and every document is explained to your satisfaction and complete understanding. The story in the Introduction illustrates one of many reasons why both personal knowledge of your estate plan and the use of qualified assistants is vital.

Acknowledgments

I owe tremendous gratitude to those who helped me acquire and distill the information required to write this book, including James E. Kirk, Christopher O'Neill, Thomas J. Horne, Ruth B. Cohen, and Caroline Hallett. Thanks also to Shirley Chavez for expert transcription and to everyone at Lowell House, especially Bud Sperry, Maria Magallanes, and Christina Ham.

The story told in the introduction is true.
The names have been changed to protect the unrepentant.

Special Note to Louisiana Residents:

Louisiana's legal system is based on the Napoleonic Code, derived from French law. This is substantially different from the law of other states. Residents of Louisiana should bear in mind that many of the legal principles discussed in this book may not apply, or may apply in a different way to your situation.

INTRODUCTION

Once upon a time, a colleague asked me to help him with some research on an estate matter. As a research lawyer, I analyze the law and prepare documents for other attorneys who represent clients directly. I don't typically work on estate cases, since they're usually pretty straightforward, requiring little in the way of legal research and paperwork once the initial plan is established. Unless there's a problem, that is.

In this case, my colleague—I'll call him Mr. Weaver, Jr.—thought the problem was minor. He needed a little research to determine the best way to correct a clerical error in a trust document, to bring it into line with a clear will he was administering as the personal representative of a deceased client's estate. No big deal, because the will was so clear and undoubtedly valid.

The client who had made the will, Mrs. Brown, was a widow without children or other close relatives. She had a couple of distant cousins in another state, whom she identified and excluded from receiving any part of her estate. She made a few small bequests to close friends and left some gifts to charities. The bulk of her estate consisted of money held in trust by a bank in a midwestern city, the same bank where her parents, and later she and her late husband, had placed their money—and their complete faith—for three-quarters of a century.

Mr. and Mrs. Brown had been close friends with the Weaver family for fifty years. The families often shared holiday celebrations and vacationed together. Mr. Weaver, Sr. was a lawyer, and had helped Mr. and Mrs. Brown with their estate planning on several occasions. Like most married couples, the Browns left the bulk of their property to each other. When Mr. Brown died, Mrs. Brown made a new will, leaving most of her estate—the money held in trust by the bank—to a charitable organization.

Some years later, Mrs. Brown decided to change her will. The Weaver family, especially Mr. Weaver, Sr., had remained her closest friends, providing her with companionship and support as she grew older. Mrs. Brown decided to make two small changes in her will: She would leave the money in trust to Mr. Weaver, Sr. instead of giving it to charity. The designated charity would receive a smaller donation. She knew that Mr. Weaver, Sr. could not assist her with this change, since he was now to be named as a beneficiary in the will, nor would it be exactly kosher for his son, Mr. Weaver, Jr. to help, since he and his father practiced law together in the same office. So she called the firm's secretary to ask her if she could retype the will with this minor change. The secretary agreed, and the new will was legally signed and witnessed.

Mrs. Brown thought her estate planning was complete: The will met all the legal requirements and expressed her intentions clearly. Her money was safely stashed in the trust account. Since the primary purpose of any legal procedure to distribute the estate of a person who has died is to carry out her intentions—referred to as "the testator's intent" when the person has made a will—this is the most important issue, and it appeared to be soundly resolved. Mr. Weaver, Sr. had been a dear friend for half a century, so he fit the legal definition of someone who is considered a "natural object of the testator's bounty." Mr. Weaver, Jr. was named personal representative of the estate, a prudent choice, since he was an attorney and son of the primary beneficiary. Like many wills, Mrs. Brown's (as well as her previous wills) contained a clause that stated: "I declare that I have distant relatives whom I do not choose to identify at this time; and I declare that I do not wish to make any such relatives beneficiaries to any extent in my Estate."

When Mrs. Brown passed away, she was in her mid-nineties. Mr. Weaver began gathering the documents to administer the estate, anticipating a simple job. However, he soon discovered that the bank had used a form for the trust document that could not have been correct—it simply didn't fit Mrs. Brown's circumstances. The trust document contained a clause called a "testamentary power of appointment." This requires the person making the trust to state who would receive the trust funds upon her death by making a specific reference to the power of appointment in the will and naming a beneficiary in that context. If the person does not do so, the trustee distributes the funds according to the state's intestacy statute—the law that determines where an individual's property will go if she dies without a valid will.

This type of trust is typically used when the maker has minor children or grandchildren, and is not certain which of these potential beneficiaries he wants to receive the property in the trust at the time he sets it up. It allows the maker to wait to see who, among several people, will most need, deserve, or otherwise be chosen to receive the money. Then he names that person as beneficiary of the trust funds when he makes or changes his will, using specific language referring to the trust.

Obviously, an error had been made. The trust document did not apply to Mrs. Brown's situation, and it plainly did not reflect her intent: to keep her money safely in trust and then pass it along as a part of her estate through the customary language used in a will. This intention was clear from both her last will and previous wills she had made. Mr. Weaver, Jr. thought it would be a simple matter of correcting the clerical error that had led the bank to use the wrong trust form.

Mr. Weaver, Jr. is a meticulous lawyer who likes to make sure all the loose ends are tied up before he closes a matter, so that his clients don't encounter problems in the future. So he asked the two cousins named in the will to sign a release stating that they would accept the terms of the will and not contest it. They agreed willingly. Then Weaver conducted a genealogical search to find out if Mrs. Brown may have had any other living relatives she didn't know about. He planned to ask these folks to sign the same kind of release of any claim against the estate, just to be sure that no problems arose in the future. This was important, because the applicable state's law did not have a provision, as many states do, limiting how distant a relative may be and still make a claim against an estate under the intestacy statutes.

Sure enough, the search turned up four cousins—excruciatingly distant cousins. They were half cousins to the fourth degree to Mrs. Brown. They lived halfway across the country. None had ever met Mrs. Brown; indeed, none were even aware of her existence. It could not have been more obvious that Mrs. Brown, a testator who specified that she had no family, did not want these folks—I'll call them, collectively, the "shirttail relations"—to receive any part of her estate.

Yet even Lewis Carroll could not have conceived a more topsy-turvy tale. When Mr. Weaver, Jr. contacted the bank to propose the legal remedies we had researched, the bankers who had been involved in creating the trust grew defensive. They vehemently insisted that such fastidious individuals as themselves could not have possibly made a mistake, and that the trust document was indeed the right one. The fact that this type of trust made no sense whatsoever for a person in Mrs. Brown's position was but a minor detail.

Enter lawyer Munson. This venomous individual taught me just how low the legal profession can sink. Smelling a fortune to be grabbed, he rallied the shirttail relations—who had previously agreed to sign documents releasing their claim to the estate of their unknown fourth-half-cousin—and convinced them to fight the will. And fight they—or he—did, with each battle reaching a new low, becoming uglier and more confusing. First, the shirttail relations filed false affidavits teeming with lies. Then Munson filed papers suggesting that Mrs. Brown's will naming Mr. Weaver, Sr. as a beneficiary was a product of "undue influence"—essentially charging that because Mr. Weaver, Sr. was a lawyer, he had abused this "power" to influence Mrs. Brown to change her will to name him as the primary beneficiary. Never mind that Mr. Weaver, Sr. was a close friend for fifty years (remember, under the law this made him a natural object of her bounty). Munson also cared little that Mr. Weaver, Sr., had also passed away by this time, and that his argument amounted to an unfounded attack on the reputation of a man no longer alive to defend his good name.

Yet disparaging the fine reputation of one dead person was not enough for the diabolical Mr. Munson. He filed papers alleging that Mrs. Brown had been susceptible to the influence of others, because she was incompetent at the time she made her will. Those who had known her testified that she was highly intelligent and strong-willed—and would have had a fit over any suggestion that she was incompetent to handle her business affairs. All the evidence pointed to the opposite conclusion—Mrs. Brown was as sharp as the proverbial tack until just days before her death, let alone several years earlier, when she had drawn up her will. Munson's argument was based upon her age alone. Ironically, Mr. Weaver Sr., who had allegedly exercised such a powerful influence over Mrs. Brown, was only a few years her junior.

The judge presiding over this matter had two duties: first and foremost, to carry out the testator's intent; and second, to hear all sides and sort out the mountain of conflicting legal arguments before him, so that he would be fair to everyone and make sure that he was, in fact, performing his primary duty to the late Mrs. Brown. As I will explain later in the book, many of Munson's legal arguments had no merit whatsoever under the applicable law. Yet he and his crew managed to muddy the water sufficiently to turn a simple matter into a complex legal quagmire.

Mr. Weaver, Jr. brought in a neutral law firm to represent Mrs. Brown's estate—a move that seemed prudent but one that effectively fanned the flames of the controversy and further eroded the money everyone was fighting over. As a result, the case dragged on for months as Munson and a gang of lawyers lined their pockets.

Though he and his clients had no case, Munson eventually "won" simply through his stubborn persistence. After several months of mounting legal bills, Mr. Weaver Jr. and his assistants concluded that continuing to fight these interlopers would, before long, completely drain the estate. He decided to reach a settlement with the shirttail relations and Munson, essentially paying them off to make them go away before more damage was done. Mrs. Brown's once-sizeable estate was ultimately reduced to a fraction of what she had wanted to leave to Mr. Weaver, Sr. and his family.

The fact that this entire fiasco was the result of a simple clerical error should have been pathetically obvious. But the bankers' scramble to cover their pin-striped posteriors by insisting that "no, mistakes do not happen at our bank"; the dastardly deeds of lawyer Munson, the true villain of this tale; the blind greed of the shirttail relations who were enticed into expecting a windfall; not to mention the well-meaning attempts of the judge to sort through the lies, accusations, and desperate pleas for justice that had been heaped before him, the bulk of the estate simply evaporated into the pockets of the sharks, vultures, and parasites.

The moral of this sad story? Estate planning is a crucial, dynamic, and ongoing process—not one static event. It pays to be skeptical, to ask questions, to check and recheck documents for errors, and to call upon expert advisers. Even a modest estate can end up somewhere other than the places the testator wants it to go if someone makes a mistake—and if a battle erupts, even a fortune can quickly disappear.

Yet, estate planning doesn't have to be a complicated, intimidating, or mysterious process. Once you understand the various steps that must be taken, where to go for good advice, and how to ask the questions that will reassure you that your estate plans are securely in place, you can gain a satisfying and reassuring command of the process. It's a matter of good financial management—both for you and your beneficiaries—so that they will never have to face the kind of nightmare scenario Mrs. Brown's intended beneficiaries were unexpectedly forced to endure.

■ Chapter 1

An Overview of Estate Planning and Why It Is So Important

A good estate plan serves two main functions: First, it helps you to effectively manage your property while you are alive, and second, it ensures that your property will go where you want it to go after your death. Estate planning is essentially a means of caring for the needs of your loved ones. Smart estate planning can also save a great deal of money, both for you and your heirs.

A will is the tool we think of most often in terms of estate planning. However, it is only one part of the complete plan most people need. A well-crafted estate plan may include insurance policies, inter vivos gifts (gifts made while the giver is still alive), pensions, trusts, and joint ownership of property with right of survivorship. All of these can be effective tools for the efficient transfer of property, both in life and after death.

More and more people are beginning to realize the benefits of estate planning. According to the American Bar Association, the number of Americans with wills grew by 50 percent between 1980 and 1995. Yet, other statistics collected by professional estate planning organizations show that approximately 70 percent of Americans today still lack even a simple will.

MY ESTATE IS SMALL— WHY BOTHER WITH A PLAN?

Everyone needs some form of estate planning. For those without much property, a simple will or trust may be enough to satisfy the bare necessities. For others, whose possessions are substantial or legally complex, a dozen or more documents may be required to accomplish the desired goals. For most of us, somewhere between these two extremes—two or three carefully crafted, yet simple steps—can achieve our objectives.

Many people mistakenly believe that estate planning is not important for younger people. It should be a part of an overall financial plan constructed by *anyone* who owns property. It is essential for those who have children.

Why spend time and money on estate planning if your property is not extensive and would already go to those you would wish to have it, by operation of the law, if you should die? There are several good reasons. The primary goals of estate planning include:

1. To be sure that your estate is transferred to those you wish to receive it upon your death.
2. To eliminate or reduce the impact of estate and other taxes on your spouse, children, and other beneficiaries.
3. To assure economical, prompt, and private distribution of your estate without the excessive involvement and expense of attorneys, courts, and others.
4. To be sure that your wishes and preferences are honored if you should become incapacitated. In most states, you can designate a personal guardian to carry out your wishes.
5. To arrange for the support, care, and needs of minor children in the event of a parent's death.
6. To reduce or eliminate the likelihood of disputes over the distribution of your estate.
7. Estate planning may be combined with savings, investment, and retirement planning, as well as long term care planning; gift-giving during your lifetime to individuals and organizations; preservation of wealth, protection of your business; and other goals.
8. Life and disability insurance is also part of an estate plan. In addition to providing for payment of your debts and the support of your family in the event of your death, these tools can help you plan for your later years.
9. As part of your plan, you choose an executor and/or trustees to carry out your directions. You can make arrangements with this person to minimize expenses, so that your estate doesn't have to pay too much in

administration costs, leaving more to those you wish to receive it.

10. Your estate plan can also provide for your funeral arrangements, so that your wishes are carried out, and the burden on your family is eased.
11. Your estate plan can benefit a charitable, educational, or religious cause, while at the same time easing the tax burdens on your estate.
12. An estate plan can help you make sure that a business you own continues to operate smoothly.
13. Estate planning also has benefits in the here and now. Some types of trusts provide current income-tax deductions. Certain components of an estate plan can serve to help plan college tuition for children or care for elderly parents.
14. The work necessary to complete an estate plan requires that you organize your records and financial life.

THE LANGUAGE OF ESTATE PLANNING

Probate and other laws that govern estate planning are filled with terminology that is often confusing, since many of the words have different meanings in other contexts, and different states may call the same thing by different names. A few common legal terms include:

1. *Administrator, executor, personal representative ("PR")*—These terms all refer to the person or institution, such as a bank

or law firm, appointed to carry out the directions and requests in a will; to collect the assets of the estate; pay the estate's debts; and distribute estate property to those entitled to receive it. In the following text, I will refer to this person as the "PR."

2. *Execute*—In reference to estate-planning documents such as wills, trusts, and powers of attorney, to execute a document means to take the legally required steps to make it official and binding, such as signing it, having it signed by witnesses, and/or having it notarized.
3. *Decedent*—A person who has died.
4. *Testate*— A person who has made a will is said to die "testate." One who has not made a will dies "intestate."
5. *Testator*—One who makes a will.
6. *Escheat*—When property reverts to the state because no one remains who is legally entitled to inherit from the decedent.
7. *Bequeath*—To transfer personal property to another person through a will. One who receives this property is said to receive a "bequest," and is called a "beneficiary," or sometimes a "legatee" or "devisee." To keep things as simple as possible, I will refer to these people throughout the book as "beneficiaries." This term also refers to those who receive property through a trust, life insurance policy, pension, or other type of transfer.
8. *Estate*—All the property owned by a person at the time of his or her death. Your "estate" includes tangibles (such as your house, cars, jewelry, and furniture), and intangibles (insurance, royalties, stocks and bonds, and bank

accounts). For some purposes, distinctions are made between the "gross estate" (everything the person owns) and the "net estate" (the gross estate less debts).

9. *Will*—A legal document a person uses to dispose of his or her property after his or her death, name a person to take care of his business, name a guardian for minor children, and, in some cases, provide for other things he or she wishes to be done after his or her death.
10. *Probate*—the court-supervised process of determining whether a will is valid or invalid, appointing a PR, identifying beneficiaries, and gathering and distributing the estate of someone who has died.
11. *Probate estate*—Property that passes through the will or is distributed according to intestacy laws, as opposed to property that passes in a different manner, such as insurance proceeds or property held in trust or joint tenancy.
12. *Residual estate*—Everything in an estate that is left after specific bequests are made. A "residuary clause," a will's catchall provision, names a person or entity that will receive all of the "rest and residue" of the estate not specifically disposed of in the will. For example, a testator may make a will that bequeaths a car to her daughter, a boat to her son, and everything else—the "rest and residue" or the residual estate—to her husband. He is the "residuary beneficiary."
13. *Heirs*—All persons, including a surviving spouse and children, who are entitled under the statutes of intestate succession to receive the property of a decedent. Sometimes "heir" is used interchangeably with "beneficiary."

14. *Next of kin*—Persons related to the decedent by blood or marriage, as set out in each state's laws.
15. *Trust*—A legal entity that owns property and serves other purposes for the benefit of the maker of the trust (also called the "trustor" or "settlor") and other beneficiaries named in the trust. There are innumerable kinds of trusts, all with different purposes.
16. *Statutes*—The written laws of a state or other jurisdiction. Each state has statutes passed by its legislature, and the United States has statutes passed by Congress.
17. *Regulations*—Written rules of a government entity, such as the IRS, that have the force and effect of law.
18. *Common law*—Also called "case law," common law refers to legal rules, requirements, and interpretations of the statutes by the higher courts through published opinions.
19. *Term life insurance*—Life insurance that will pay a death benefit to a beneficiary in the policy if the person insured dies while the policy is in effect (during the "term" of the policy).
20. *Permanent life insurance*—Any of several types of life insurance (sometimes called "whole life" or "universal life") that, in addition to paying a death benefit, provides a return on the money paid in as premiums, after a certain period of time has elapsed.
21. *Power of attorney*—A document that gives another person the authority to act on the maker's behalf with regard to certain matters spelled out in the document. A "durable power of attorney" is one that authorizes a named person to make specific decisions (usually

health-care and financial matters) if the maker becomes incapacitated and can no longer make these decisions for herself or himself.

22. *Living will*—A document that indicates what type of life-sustaining measures the maker does or does not wish to be taken on his or her behalf if he or she becomes incapacitated, and under what circumstances.

PREPARING FOR THE ESTATE-PLANNING PROCESS

You can save yourself a great deal of time, money, delay, and aggravation if you complete certain tasks before you meet with an attorney, financial planner, or other professional. The key to good preparation involves a process of locating documents, amassing knowledge, and framing questions. In reading this book, you have taken the first step toward gaining an overview of the principles of estate planning, which will enable you to make a preliminary assessment of your circumstances and the options that may be right for your situation.

In formulating an estate plan, your goals and wishes as to how you would like your property to be managed during your life and disposed of after your death should be your first priority. In addition to the practical chores, this requires some soul-searching as you consider your family and the needs of its members, friends you may wish to benefit, and other personal concerns. You may also have unique issues to think about, such as providing for a child with special needs, making sure a pet will be cared for, or planning for the continued operation of a family business. As you begin to consider creating your estate plan, think about the following preliminary questions. Some you can probably answer immediately, while others may require careful thought and discussion with your spouse, family members, or your professional advisers:

1. What types of property do you own or hold an ownership interest in? What kind of interest do you have? Sole ownership, partnership interests, joint tenancy?
2. Who would you like to be the guardian of your minor children if you and your spouse both die before they are raised?
3. Who should administer your estate after your death?
4. Will your estate be subject to federal estate or other taxes? If so, what can you do to eliminate or minimize taxes?
5. How will the person administering your estate pay for such taxes if any are due?
6. Will the probate process in your state be complex and expensive?
7. How should you and your spouse hold title to your real estate and other significant assets?
8. If you cannot care for yourself, whom do you choose to take care of you, make decisions about your health care, and manage your financial affairs?

9. How do you want to be cared for if you become incapacitated?
10. If you cannot manage your estate and other business affairs, whom do you want to take over?
11. Should you prepare a will, a living trust, or both?
12. Whom do you want to receive your possessions upon your death?
13. Who should receive the proceeds of your life insurance, retirement accounts, and other benefits after your death?
14. What is your estate's value?

The latter factor can be both important and tricky to assess. The net value of a person's estate—the figure that determines what type of probate procedure applies and whether your estate is subject to taxes—is generally determined by starting with the fair-market value of all your assets, then subtracting your debts, including home mortgages. Before you formulate your estate plan, you may need to have certain assets appraised. This can be important in determining whether, and to what extent, your estate will be taxed after your death and what resources you would have available should you become incapacitated.

What Do You Own?

One of the first and most essential steps in estate planning is to have a clear picture of what you own, how you own it, and its approximate value. This sounds simple, but people are often unaware of the true nature or extent of their property. For example, the home you purchased twenty years ago may have tripled in value. The truck you received in your divorce settlement may still be subject to a lien by one of your ex-spouse's creditors. Ever watch the PBS program, "The Antiques Road Show"? People are often astonished to learn that the pretty little spice cabinet they picked up for five bucks at a garage sale is in fact a Georgian rarity worth ten thousand dollars.

Sometimes confusion arises because people believe that they own a piece of property, when in fact, they don't. This may include real estate mortgaged for an amount that exceeds its value; bank accounts that contain less than the liabilities the money would pay off; or a piece of property held in joint ownership, under a legal principal, such as the law governing property owned by married couples. It is vital to sort out these issues before you can have a clear picture of what type of estate plan you need.

Getting Organized

For any estate planning endeavor, it is necessary to review your property, debts, insurance policies, and other documents. As an initial step, locate and organize the following documents and information (you may wish to make copies of key documents, such as deeds and titles, and leave the originals where you generally keep them, to avoid the risk of losing essential items):

1. Deeds and titles to property, such as real estate, vehicles, trailers, etc.
2. Appraisals or your own best estimates of the present worth of valuable personal property, such as jewelry, antiques, or art.
3. All insurance policies, including life, health, and property.
4. All estate planning documents you have executed, including wills, trust documents, and contracts relating to inheritances, etc.
5. Financial statements, information on bank accounts, trusts, credit unions, and other financial records, as well as information about your debts.
6. Stock certificates, bonds, other investments, and broker information.
7. Retirement, pension, profit-sharing, and other deferred benefit accounts or plans.
8. Tax returns for the past few years.
9. Records on any business you own or in which you hold an interest.
10. Other records, documents, or information that may have an impact upon your estate-planning needs. For instance, a patent on an invention that brings you royalties or licensing fees; a premarital agreement with your spouse; rental property that produces income; a child who will need long-term medical care. These factors will affect the options you must consider when setting up your estate plan.
11. Names and addresses of family members; friends you may wish to include in your will; charitable organizations you would like to assist; physicians, attorneys, financial advisers, stockbrokers; and banks where you hold accounts.

Does this seem overwhelming? Several steps may help. First, if your records are extremely disorganized, don't try to tackle a major reorganizing project in a single day. Work on it a little at a time. For instance, set aside a couple of hours every Saturday morning for a month or two to devote to the task. Second, consider creating a "panic book" or "hurricane box." Estate-planning attorney Merri Rudd describes a client who came to her with his important documents and key information consolidated in a notebook he called a "panic book," with pockets for copies of important documents, such as deeds. Financial planner Judy Lawrence once had a Florida client who kept the same materials and information in a steel strongbox she stored near her front door, so that she could grab it quickly if she had to evacuate. Whatever method you choose, it's important to keep all this information together in order to formulate a comprehensive estate plan.

If you simply can't face this job on your own, consider working with a professional organizer. They know the methods to help even the most scattered get organized, often for a surprisingly affordable fee. Check your telephone directory, or contact the National Association of Professional Organizers (see Appendix) for a referral.

What Does Creating an Estate Plan Involve?

Once you have the necessary information and records, the initial establishment of an estate plan won't be a complex or difficult process. While some of the options discussed later in this book are admittedly complicated, most people do not require such sophisticated techniques—and if you are in a position to benefit from these options, it is well worth the time and expense involved to learn about them and seek the professional assistance required to take advantage of them. But if your estate is fairly small and relatively simple, you can do a good deal of the preliminary work on your own and then seek the assistance of a lawyer (and, if necessary, other professional advisers) to put everything into its correct form. It is important to remember that an estate plan can be adjusted, usually without too much effort and expense, if your needs change.

The horror story provided in the introduction shows why it is essential to review all your documents yourself, to ask questions, and be sure you understand everything even the most trusted professionals have set up for you. If your estate is more complex, you can still do a lot of the initial work before you seek the counsel of your attorney, insurance professionals, accountant, and/or financial planner. The background work necessary for a good estate plan may also require the input of others, such as appraisers, and, though the thought makes many of us cringe, family members. The idea of sitting down and discussing where your property will go upon your death may hold little appeal, but you stand to gain considerable peace of mind in having such matters squared away.

EDUCATE YOURSELF

Books

Books such as this one, and the others listed in the Appendix, can help you arm yourself with the knowledge you need to work with your advisers to make the most informed choices for your situation. The information I have outlined here is necessarily broad, and it is my goal to provide an overview of many of the estate-planning choices available today—not detailed, in-depth guidelines on any particular option.

Some of the books and organizations I have listed in the Appendix provide more specific information on particular issues in estate planning, and I urge you to seek more detailed sources of knowledge on matters of interest to you. Be aware, however, of two important provisos as you gather information. First, the laws and regulations that govern estate planning and related fields, especially tax laws, are changing rapidly. Also, the case law or common law of each state—the law as applied and established by court decisions—literally evolves every day as the higher courts hand down new opinions. A book that is several years old may contain outdated information about specific laws or regulations.

Second, some of the books I have listed contain helpful tools, such as charts and checklists to help you organize and analyze information, but then advise you to try to create even complex trusts without a lawyer's assistance. Please forgive me if I harp on this, but I have seen too many disasters arise from wee mistakes in the simplest of documents. Bookstores abound with volumes of do-it-yourself forms, and many states now have their own form books specifically designed to meet their requirements for the pertinent will and trust documents. Nolo Press, a publishing company devoted to self-help legal materials, publishes a series of such form books (some of these are listed in the Appendix). So you may be able to do *nearly* all of your estate planning work yourself—but always have your plan reviewed by a competent professional, and realize that if he tells you that it must be redone, he does so for your protection.

Attorneys differ on their opinions of such "do-it-yourself" legal tools. Attorney James E. Kirk, referring specifically to financial planner Norman Dacey's popular book *How to Avoid Probate!* states, "Some of the forms are very simplified, but that may be okay. An attorney may want to turn a two-page document into a ten-page document, but that's just attorneys. Sometimes a two-page document will do." Attorney Ruth B. Cohen adds, "I don't discourage people from bringing in forms they've done themselves, but I generally prefer that they don't."

Some estate planning lawyers believe that while such forms may be valuable tools to help people gather and organize the details they need for estate planning, each individual estate plan requires specialized attention from a competent attorney. "Sometimes clients bring in forms they have completed and ask me to simply review and rubber-stamp them" one attorney remarked. "I don't feel I can do that. Forms are fine as a source of information, but each will or trust document needs to be drafted to meet the individual's needs."

If you wish to complete a portion of your own estate-planning documents, discuss your intention with an attorney *before* you spend a great deal of time at work on this process. Some supply potential clients with their own checklists and instructions, which are faster and easier to use than many of the standardized forms for gathering and organizing information.

If you have completed a form from a book and believe it is complete and correct but the lawyer you consult tells you it needs to be longer, different, or more complex, ask why. Some lawyers do make things needlessly complex, while others, hopefully most, are truly looking out for your best interests, one of the main components of their duty to you. What appears to be churning may in fact be vital work that must be done to protect your rights and property.

You should realize that lawyers and other professionals must protect themselves, too. One who carelessly rubber-stamps a document prepared by a client, which later fails to meet legal requirements or do what it is supposed to do, can be subject to malpractice suits or disciplinary sanctions by the state. These can range from public censure to loss of license to practice. The attorney or financial planner who insists on taking the time to thoroughly review your documents and, if necessary, change or redo them, is only obeying the requirements of her profession—and doing the job you have asked her to do.

Seminars

Many community groups, attorneys, and public service organizations offer workshops and seminars on estate planning. Some are general, others focus on specific topics, such as living trusts or the estate-planning concerns of certain groups, for example, those with family-owned businesses, or nontraditional couples. Local probate or elder law attorneys, senior citizens advocacy groups, and state agencies on aging often conduct estate-planning and related workshops for seniors, and can also offer referrals to attorneys and other professionals who specialize in both estate planning and elder law.

Many of the seminars are single-session classes provided are free or at a modest cost; others may run several days and charge a substantial fee. Proceed with caution if you are considering one of the more expensive seminars. Some are presented by reputable companies and provide valuable information, but others are outright scams. Reports have surfaced over the past few years of companies that sell "do-it- yourself" living trust kits through high-priced seminars aimed at senior citizens. These unscrupulous groups charge far more than an experienced attorney would bill for drafting an individualized estate plan, and the information can be inaccurate. Investigate the company or individual sponsoring or presenting any fee-based seminar before you sign on, and if you smell a rat, contact your state's attorney general's office, a consumer rights group, or senior services organization.

Software

An increasing number of inexpensive software programs have become available in recent years to assist people in completing their own legal work. Like books, software can be a helpful tool to assist you in organizing information, crunching numbers, and preparing draft documents. But forgive me if I sound like a broken record: No software program, no matter how sophisticated or detailed, can take the place of qualified professional advisers. Use software to gather data and, if you wish, to draft the documents you believe you need, then take what you have prepared to your advisers. Sometimes, with a good program, this can save you money, because it enables you to present an attorney or other professional well-organized, carefully processed information that requires minimal adjustment.

Many attorneys now use software systems to assist them in preparing your estate planning documents. This can shave hours off the time needed to perform calculations on tax-liability issues, for example, as well as save time and money on completing documents. Software designed for attorneys tends to be highly interactive and more complex than that sold in the "do-it-yourself" kits, so if your attorney mentions using software, it is probably to your advantage—he is not, as some may assume, simply doing something you could just as easily have done yourself.

The Internet

During the past few years, the Internet has emerged as a vast and comprehensive source of information on every imaginable topic, including estate planning. Today, having an on-line computer is akin to having a desktop library. For those with access to cyberspace, Web sites devoted to estate, trust, and probate issues can provide information on local and national laws, sources of professional assistance, publications, discussion and news groups, and other resources.

If you are not on-line through a computer at home or at work, check with your local public library. Many libraries now have computers patrons may use to access the Internet, as well as free classes on how to navigate your way through cyberspace. (Most people can learn the basics in an hour or two.)

Various legal organizations, law firms, individual attorneys, legal publishers, and government offices maintain excellent Web sites. For example, the U.S. House of Representatives has an "Internet Law Library" with links to state and federal laws, court rules, cases, and articles on a plethora of topics, including estate planning. The American Bar Association has an excellent Web site with extensive information and many links to other sites.

Various organizations composed of estate-planning attorneys and other professionals who work in the field also have sites that provide local referrals, news on recent changes in the law, articles, and a diverse array of links.

A selection of Web sites that contain information, provide referrals, or are of general interest on estate-planning topics is listed in the Appendix. Internet addresses change frequently, so if the URLs provided in this book are incorrect, a search using the name of the organization or government office usually leads you to the right site.

Bear in mind that anyone can create a Web site, and some of the information may be inaccurate or inflammatory. I have seen many Web sites that provide extremely helpful information, as well as a few with terrible advice. Weigh what you read on the Web or in print against your own common sense, and always consider the source.

CHOOSING AN ATTORNEY

No matter what type of estate plan you create, you should eventually involve an attorney. Most attorneys in general practice are perfectly capable of drawing up a basic will or simple living trust, and can provide other estate-planning advice for people whose estates are small and uncomplicated. However, if your estate is more complex, you may need to consult an attorney who specializes in estate planning or "probate law," as it is sometimes called. Some are also certified public accountants, and those who are not generally have a network of other professionals they work with as needed, such as accountants, financial planners, elder law specialists, and insurance experts.

When you choose an attorney to assist you in creating the important documents that will become a part of your estate plan, pick someone you are comfortable working with. He should be willing to discuss options, answer questions, and address your concerns. Be prepared to reveal intimate details about your family and finances. Even though this information remains confidential, it is important to feel at ease in discussing such details with him.

Also, choose a lawyer who is well versed and experienced in the issues involved in estate planning. The same attorney who handled your divorce so well or was so good at untangling that complicated real estate transfer may or may not be the right person to help with your estate planning. More and more, today's lawyers specialize in one area of law, or several interrelated fields (such as tax, probate, and real estate).

The best way to find a good estate planning lawyer is to ask friends and family members for referrals to attorneys who have helped them plan their estates to their satisfaction. If this is not an option, most states, along with some larger cities, have lawyer referral services sponsored by the state bar association or other attorney groups. Check your telephone directory, or call the local or state bar association. Many of the professional organizations listed in the Appendix have referral services or membership lists that can be accessed by the Internet, telephone, or mail.

Do realize that most bar association referral services allow any licensed lawyer to register for referrals in a certain area of law, and because someone is referred as an estate planning attorney does not guarantee any particular level of expertise or experience. Likewise, the professional organizations for estate planning attorneys (see Appendix) vary tremendously in their membership requirements, from nomination and election by top professional colleagues to a lawyer's simply paying a fee to join. Referral services are a good place to start but offer no guarantee that the attorney referred will be the best person for you to hire.

In contrast, states that recognize a legal specialization in estate planning may issue a title such as "board certified specialist." These certifications usually require that fairly high standards have been met, such as proof that an attorney has spent a specific number of years devoting a stated percentage of his practice to estate planning work.

Ask the Right Questions

Even if an attorney comes with glowing recommendations and board certification, make sure you take time to ask questions before making the decision to hire her to complete your estate plan. Find out how much of her practice is devoted to estate planning, how long she has been working in the field, and how her fees are structured (i.e., flat fee, hourly, or otherwise).

Many attorneys charge a set fee for preparing a basic will and related estate planning documents, such as a durable power of attorney and a living will. This fee generally covers consultation and information gathering, the process of drawing up the documents, and the execution and filing of the will and other papers. It should also cover the time required to explain the documents to you, so that you fully understand the terms, as well as answer any simple questions at a later date if they arise. Other attorneys charge an hourly fee, in which case your own efforts to prepare and organize the documents and information necessary for your estate plan can save you a bundle. Attorney's fees vary tremendously, depending upon geographic location, the lawyer's years of experience and level of expertise, as well as innumerable other factors.

Your attorney should be willing to work with you to help keep her fees reasonable. For example, at or before your first meeting, she generally gives you a checklist or assignment of information to gather, documents to locate, and other tasks to accomplish. Some give clients an estate planning fact sheet with information on everything they need to locate or find out before the first meeting, including a form to be mailed back before the first face-to-face meeting, if possible. That way, the attorney has a chance to review it in advance, so that the time of both attorney and client is used more efficiently.

Many attorneys employ paralegals or legal assistants to draft the initial documents according to instructions the lawyer provides after meeting with you. Then your lawyer reviews them to make sure they are complete and accurate. This can be a good way to keep the fees reasonable, as long as the attorney takes the time to carefully check the documents after her assistant has completed them.

No lawyer should charge you for a brief, initial telephone interview. If someone refuses to answer preliminary questions before scheduling a session in which fees will be charged, or asks for a retainer before he will even speak with you, walk away. You need certain information before you hire an attorney, including an overview of his background and experience in estate planning; a brief description of the types of services you need and whether he provides such services; whether he charges a retainer fee; how his fees are structured (flat-fee package or hourly rates); and how long he expects it will take to complete your estate plan. You may also wish to ask about his policy on returning telephone calls (this can be a source of great frustration and misunderstanding); whether you need to bring documents to the first session; how often he bills you; and how soon you are expected to pay. It sometimes takes several attempts to find someone you will be comfortable working with, so do not hesitate to call several lawyers before you make a final decision. (Lawyers are accustomed to this and won't be offended.)

Even if your estate planning requires only the execution of a simple will, it generally takes at least two meetings with an attorney, after the introductory conversation, to complete the process. Often, during the first meeting, your attorney outlines all the information that must be gathered, discusses the options available to you, and explains what documents must be drafted, such as a will, trust, or others. Then he draws up the documents and arranges a second meeting in which you review them. If you are satisfied that the documents reflect your intentions and you fully understand how they work, they can be signed and filed, and the process has been essentially completed. Naturally, a more complex estate plan requires more time and effort.

Obtaining Low-Cost or Free Legal Assistance

In some places, pro bono (free) legal services are available to help those who cannot afford to hire a lawyer to assist them with their estate plan. Senior citizens are often eligible for these services through volunteer attorney programs, elder service organizations, and other programs. The Young Lawyer's Division of the American Bar Association offers such assistance through some of its local chapters, and many state or local bar associations have similar programs, both for seniors and for younger people with limited income. Check with local legal aid offices, bar associations, senior service providers, local libraries, law schools, or the national groups listed in the Appendix to learn what is available in your area. The American Bar Association has a Web site, as do some of the other organizations I have listed, to provide information and referrals.

Some attorneys bill their fees on a sliding scale according to the client's income. Others take a certain number of pro bono clients each year to satisfy licensing requirements or their own sense of duty (sometimes such clients must be referred by a state bar program or social service agency). If you need to know about these options, be sure to ask about this the first time you speak with an attorney.

CHOOSING OTHER PROFESSIONAL ADVISERS

People can begin with other professionals in formulating an estate plan. You may learn from your tax accountant that you face a potential estate tax problem, or your life insurance agent might suggest certain steps you should take to organize a better plan. For those with substantial assets or complex investments, a financial planner might be the first person consulted. Most people need to work with at least two of these professionals in completing a comprehensive estate plan.

Christopher M. O'Neill, a financial planner and investment adviser representative, works with clients interested in various planning techniques, including charitable giving plans, to achieve income-tax and estate planning benefits. Such financial planning services, for example, are offered through W. S. Griffith and Co., Inc., a registered investment adviser. He advises those seeking a qualified financial planner to begin by asking for referrals. "Seek someone with a good reputation, then come armed with appropriate questions," he suggests. "Seek background information, do some reading on the topic you want to discuss, and learn some of the language and options available, so that you can ask questions about the techniques that interest you."

O'Neill also emphasizes that clients should not expect "one-stop shopping" in terms of finding one professional who can handle all aspects of a complex estate plan, or a financial adviser who can provide all the answers and advice a client needs in a single session. "Don't expect to get specific advice without going through a process whereby your entire financial picture is examined. The planner has an obligation to do the necessary discovery and analysis before he can offer any recommendations. It would be professionally irresponsible to provide specific recommendations without conducting a thorough fact-finding effort, perhaps even a full financial plan, depending upon the goals and preferences of the client. This is an obligation, especially when we're using advanced estate planning techniques," he notes.

How involved this process is depends upon the client's previous financial experiences and goals. "The starting point of any process is the definition of goals and objectives. Estate planning is a subset of financial planning," O'Neill explains. "Even if a client is strictly interested in estate planning efforts, we still need to focus on a broad range of information, but there is less emphasis on the more traditional aspects of full-scale financial planning, such as cash-flow analysis."

In O'Neill's practice, he generally schedules an initial meeting to determine the client's goals and objectives and to see whether his services will be meaningful for the client. He follows this up with a second meeting focused on information gathering. "It's essential to get the raw data together and look at the numbers," he explains. "But it is equally important to clarify the client's objectives. People often come in, aware that they have an estate tax problem, combined with a charitable intent, but don't know where to go from there—they simply want help. We go through a detailed question-and-answer process to pin down the individual's specific goals. This can be one of the side benefits of the financial planning process."

O'Neill adds that this process, like the work done with an attorney, may involve answering personal questions. "Make sure that you choose someone with whom you can enjoy a comfortable working relationship," he advises. "You should be confident that the person is competent, ethical, and will be able to address your concerns."

Financial planners may qualify for certain professional designations, including the title of Certified Financial Planner (CFP®). However, unlike attorneys, who must pass a bar exam in order to be licensed to practice law, financial planners are not required to hold the CFP® license, and many highly qualified individuals do not. Yet, a CFP® designation indicates that they have demonstrated certain basic knowledge in key fields, including estate planning. "Estate planning is one of five courses that is required to sit for the CFP® exam, and CFPs are required to fulfill certain continuing education requirements," O'Neill explains. "So someone who holds the CFP® designation should be qualified in this area, but the title is no guarantee that a person is qualified to provide advice on any specific area of estate planning. Likewise, not all good financial planners are CFPs."

O'Neill notes that two organizations, the International Association of Financial Planners (IAFP) and the Institute of Certified Financial Planners (ICFP), provide direct referral services that can help people locate financial planners in their area (see Appendix).

Use caution in choosing a professional financial adviser, urges insurance and investment professional Caroline Hallett. "Beware of those with a 'one-size-fits-all' mentality, she advises. "I am surprised at some of the people who claim to be experts. A person should not call themselves a financial planner or financial adviser unless they have the credentials. Specific training is essential for different types of financial expertise, and the certifications require different tests. For example, a Certified Financial Planner and a Certified Life Underwriter (CLU) require different testing."

Hallett, like O'Neill, emphasizes the importance of educating yourself and gathering enough information to make a good decision before committing your resources to a particular plan. "Choose an adviser who is willing to sit down with you for an initial consultation in which you can trade information and decide if you want to go into the planning stage," she advises. "There should not be a fee for this initial consultation. A good financial representative begins with a question-and-answer session designed to try to arrive at the potential client's goals for the future. This is the most important step, and should include a willingness to educate the client enough, so that he is able to tell the financial representative what these goals are. The adviser should also examine the client's risk tolerance, and complete a confidential analysis as a result of the question-and-answer session. In this analysis, the adviser should be able to assist the client in coming up with a road map that tracks his financial life from the present to retirement," she explains.

Hallett advises clients seeking investment assistance to choose a financial adviser who represents a reputable broker/dealer. "Advisers should be licensed through a company such as the Principal Financial Group, Dean Witter, or Merrill Lynch. Many of these companies have a specific process their representatives follow to help the client arrive at a plan. It's like putting together a puzzle," she notes.

The time and complexity of this process depend upon the individual and his goals, she adds. "Generally, it takes about three appointments. But for those with more complex financial lives, involving extensive assets and, for example, several trusts, more time and specialized advisers, such as security specialists, may need to become involved in the process."

Most professionals work as a part of a team, so they can involve others with different skills and training when their expertise is required. "When I work with clients who are structuring their investments as a part of an estate plan," says Hallett, "I always work with accountants and attorneys in the process. The attorney specifies what type of trust is appropriate for the client, and the accountant provides financial information."

Hallett's choice of partners depends upon the needs of each client. "For example, someone who comes to me with a plan that involves investing money from the sale of a home faces capital-gains tax and other major tax consequences. I work closely with accountants in this type of situation, along with security specialists and other professionals."

THE MOST IMPORTANT COMPONENT OF ESTATE PLANNING: UNDERSTANDING WHAT YOU ARE DOING AND WHY

Seeking sound advice is not the same as relinquishing control of your estate and the components that go into planning it. Always bear in mind that your advisers are there to help you achieve your goals—and to make sure you know exactly what that process involves. Never allow someone to talk you into following a plan you do not feel is right, or one you do not understand. A good professional adviser is always willing to take the time to explain why she is suggesting that you take a particular step, what the step should accomplish, and how it is supposed to further your goals. Don't be afraid to ask questions, and keep asking until they are answered thoroughly. Insist that complex matters be explained to you in terms you can understand, and if any professional is unwilling or unable to do so, seek the advice of someone who will.

Attorney Thomas J. Horne was once called upon to represent a client in a fearsome will battle that occurred as the result of both the professionals' and the client's failure to carefully read and understand the documents that comprised her estate plan, and how they worked together. As a result, the validity of the entire estate-distribution scheme faced a challenge. "This client placed her full trust in her bankers and her attorneys," he recalls. "The trust the bank had set up for her functioned as it was supposed to during her lifetime: She received her monthly check, so she never questioned it. Nobody on either end reviewed the trust documents once they had been set up but assumed that everything was all right. The client should have requested that an approved copy of the trust be returned to her after the agreement was executed, then sat down with her lawyer and gone over it."

Horne urges his clients never to sign anything they don't understand. "I recall one of my law school professors reminding us that as attorneys, people trust us with their lives and their assets. He told us we should follow this principle in dealing with our clients: 'If you don't understand, it cannot happen.' This is essential, because mistakes happen. It is so much better to eliminate the problem before you get into it. Probate is not a good place for litigation. Will contests are the nastiest cases in the world."

Horne advises clients to take whatever time is necessary to review all aspects of their estate plan. "Get a copy of each and every document that is a part of your estate plan, then sit down with your lawyer, with all the documents in front of you. If you don't understand every bit of it, ask questions until you do. You may even need to revoke and redo certain documents. If this is necessary to create a comprehensive plan that is clear to you, don't hesitate. Do this whenever you create a new trust, for example, or change any part of your plan. Make your adviser structure things in words you understand. If you can't get an immediate explanation, insist that the document be redone."

Chapter 2

The Laws That Govern Estate Planning

Most of us are familiar with a few of the fundamental laws and tools involved in the estate planning process. We all know about wills and life insurance policies, have an idea of what the probate laws cover, and more and more people are learning about and using various types of trusts. Yet, as the laws change and innovative new methods of protecting and distributing property develop, many people are not aware of new options that may be available.

Each state has both statutory (the written code enacted by the legislature) and common (court-made) laws that directly or indirectly govern estate planning. Most states have adopted some form of the Uniform Probate Code, and all have a set of laws governing the distribution of estates. Other laws, too, impact estate planning, including marital property laws, federal and state tax laws, and trust requirements.

WHAT IS PROBATE?

Probate is a court-supervised legal procedure for wrapping up a person's affairs and distributing his property after he dies. If someone dies with a will, or dies "intestate" (with no will or other estate planning provisions, such as a living trust), their estate goes through probate. (Trusts, forms of co-ownership, and other means for distributing property after death without involving the probate court are discussed later in the book.) In every legal jurisdiction in America, a special court handles cases involving the administration of estates. Most of these are called probate courts. Some jurisdictions may give them different names, such as "chancery" courts.

The probate process determines whether a will is valid; seeks to discover from the will what the testator (the maker of the will) intended to happen to his property; and carries out that intent by gathering and distributing the assets. For those who die intestate, the probate court oversees the distribution of their property according to the applicable law.

When there is a will, the court's primary goal in supervising the probate procedure is to determine and carry out the testator's intent. This is usually accomplished by reviewing papers filed with the court, which indicate that the legally required steps have been taken and the decedent's property has been distributed according to the instructions in the will. Formal hearings or other courtroom proceedings are generally only required when a problem arises, such as an ambiguous will or a lawsuit contesting the will.

The cost of probating an estate varies according to the state, and the size and complexity of the estate, as well as the efficiency of the planning. Generally, a smaller and simpler estate costs less to probate than a larger one. The administration costs associated with probating an estate are always paid out of its assets. Even larger estates can minimize probate costs by using legal devices such as joint tenancy and trusts to take out of the estate all or most property that would have to go through the probate process.

PROBATE LAW

Probate laws govern how a person's property will pass to others at the time of her death, as well as set the legal requirements for how this will be accomplished. Property passes in three basic ways: by will; through alternatives to a will, such as trusts; or by intestacy. An individual's personal property passes according to the law of the place where the person lives at the time of her death. Real estate passes according to the law of the state where the property is located.

All state laws allow for a simplified probate procedure for certain estates, often called "informal" probate. Sometimes informal probate is limited to estates with a total value that is less than a specific amount. In some states, the informal process cannot be used where real estate is involved in the probate. In others, even very large estates, if well planned, you can take advantage of the simplified, less expensive probate procedure.

Some states take this process a step further, by completely exempting smaller estates from probate. Through the use of what is often called an affidavit procedure, beneficiaries designated to inherit property can simply complete an affidavit (a written statement signed under oath). The affidavit—plus other documents that may be required by the state, such as a copy of the will—is then presented to the person or institution holding the property, which is then turned over to the beneficiary.

State probate laws may also contain special provisions to make things easier for the decedent's survivors. For example, the law may allow certain assets to be transferred immediately to a surviving spouse, without waiting for the probate process to be completed. Such assets may include the family homestead, basic personal effects, and the decedent's last paycheck.

Probate statutes also attempt to deal with common problems. For example, the statute may provide that property given to a beneficiary by the testator during his lifetime will not be treated as an advance against that person's inheritance, unless the decedent had declared in writing that the gift was to be construed as such, or the heir has acknowledged in writing that the gift was, in fact, an advancement on inheritance.

Probate law also attempts to protect the right of an individual to determine who is to receive his assets at the time of death; it also protects the person's surviving spouse's and children's rights to receive some property to contribute to their support.

Laws of Intestacy

Those who do not have a will or other distribution system, such as a living trust, at the time of death are said to die "intestate." In this case, a section of the state's probate laws determines where the person's estate will go—to their "heirs" as defined by the law. These laws are based on blood relation alone, as noted in the introduction, along with marriage. As we've seen, squabbles over property are not uncommon, even when the person who died had a will, trust, and what they believe to be a sound estate plan. Disputes are even more likely to arise when someone dies without a will. The laws vary, but most divide the estate among the decedent's spouse, children, and parents , or, if they are dead, among siblings or other relatives.

Intestacy statutes may also be invoked when a will is found to be void, or a court declares a portion of a valid will void. The latter is called partial intestacy. Also, if a will and other documents do not dispose of all the testator's property, then those designated as heirs under the intestacy law receive the property. This may be true even if the will's specific language disinherits the person. In some states, if the will is not filed for probate within a specific number of years, the court is required to distribute the estate according to intestacy law.

Intestate distribution may be simple or complex, depending on the decedent's family. For example, if a person dies leaving a spouse and one or more children who do not have children of their own, the law generally distributes their estate to these family members, according to a mathematical formula of division that is specified in the statute. The portion of the estate allotted to the surviving spouse depends upon other laws governing property within the marriage relationship. For example, in New Mexico, a community property state, the decedent's share of the community property owned by the couple automatically passes to the surviving spouse, so he becomes the owner of all property formerly held by both as community property (similar to the right of survivorship under joint tenancy). Separate property is divided among the spouse and surviving children, with the spouse taking one-quarter of separate property, and the children receiving three-quarters of this type of property.

The laws distributing property to surviving children and other relatives use different formulas to divide the property. For example, under a "per capita" system, the heirs are counted and then the estate is divided equally among them. In some states, this is applied only if all the "issue" (descendants) of the decedent are of the same degree of kinship and are living; for example, his children. If one of the decedent's children has died, but she left children of her own, these grandchildren divide the part of the estate that would have gone to the deceased child (in this case, their mother).

Intestacy statutes also provide for more distant relatives to divide the estate when there is no surviving spouse or issue—as in the example in the introduction. Kindred of half-blood are generally allowed to inherit the same share they would receive if they were of full-blood. In some states, however, relatives of half-blood take a one-half share, or receive property only if there are no full-blood relatives of the same degree. The statutes also provide for children born after the person dies, and adopted children, who generally inherit in the same manner as natural children born before the person's death. State probate codes also contain a requirement that heirs must survive the decedent by a set number of hours. This can come into play when, for example, several members of a family are killed in an accident.

Probating an estate without a will can be tricky, as well as more expensive. It may require the PR to conduct a search for missing or unknown heirs, and assets are often tied up while the court, PR, and attorneys try to sort out where monies and property should go. In some states, those of more distant kinship to the decedent (for example, more distant than first cousins), cannot inherit even if there are no other living relatives. This may seem harsh, but it helps avoid ludicrous scenarios like that related in this book's introduction.

If no relatives eligible to inherit can be located, the entire estate "escheats" to the state. There is a common myth that whenever someone dies without a will, the estate is subject to escheat. This is false, because all states have intestacy statutes (as described above) to distribute the estate to relatives. Escheat only occurs when there is no will *and* no family, or no family closely related enough to claim the estate. (This varies by state. Some have limits, some don't.)

Spouse/Child Allowance Laws

State probate codes usually include what is called a "family allowance" and a "personal property allowance." This is often a set sum of money, such as $10,000. The family allowance is exempt from and has priority over all other claims—by creditors or others—against the estate. It is provided in addition to the spouse's intestate share or any amount provided by a will. The family allowance cannot, in some states, be reached at all by creditors of the estate. The surviving spouse may also be entitled to receive personal property valued at a certain amount, for example, $3,500. This allowance is made in addition to the family allowance.

To protect the surviving spouse, most states have laws that limit one spouse's right to disinherit the other. These laws state that a surviving spouse has the right to receive a certain portion of the deceased partner's property, no matter what that person provided in a will or intended. In most cases, these laws have no effect when one spouse has arranged to leave the other at least half of his property.

It is important to remember that certain types of property cannot be transferred in a will. Retirement benefits, property held in joint tenancy, certain types of bank accounts, and life insurance must be transferred by naming a beneficiary in the document that governs ownership of this property, such as a deed or insurance policy. Be sure that any property you own in one of these arrangements is set up correctly, so the person you wish to receive it when you die will do so.

OTHER STATUTORY LAW

In addition to the laws specifically governing probate, estates are also affected by other state and federal laws, including family or marital laws, homestead statutes, tax laws, banking laws, and others, depending on the estate. (Some of the laws that often impact estate planning are outlined in more detail later.)

Special Concerns for Married People

The states follow one of two rules affecting ownership of property acquired during a marriage. There are two basic systems, a majority "common law" or "marital property" system in which the owner of the property is usually determined simply by the name that appears on the ownership document. However, eight states still follow "community property" systems, in which most property acquired during a marriage is owned equally by both spouses. Thus, a wife who buys a car in her own name in a marital property state is the car's sole owner, while a wife who buys a car in her own name in a community-property state owns only half interest in that vehicle. The other half is owned by her husband, unless the couple agrees otherwise and uses specific language in the written ownership documents.

State laws that govern the property owned by a husband and wife, such as community-property laws, may affect joint tenancy and other forms of property ownership. For example, in community-property states, all property acquired after the marriage—with a few exceptions—is presumed to be community property in which each spouse has an equal half interest. Those legally imposed presumptions can usually be changed where both parties agree that the change is desirable, but this typically requires a written agreement if it is to be valid. When people move from a marital-property state to a community-property state, or vice versa, their ownership scheme can become confusing. Married couples should discuss their property status and ownership options with their attorney.

Debt and Creditors

When you die, your estate will be responsible for paying any debts you owed. Your PR (or, if you had a living trust, your trustee) will take care of this task. While some types of property cannot be reached by creditors, as discussed later, most people want to be sure that their estate will be able to pay all their legitimate obligations, both as a matter of ethics, and for the convenience of the PR, who will have to negotiate a settlement with creditors if there are insufficient assets in the estate to meet all of its debts. This is one of the main purposes of life insurance.

People sometimes worry that if the estate is left with more debts than assets, their heirs or beneficiaries will be required to pay. This is not true, with one exception: If you leave an estate that is subject to federal estate taxes, this debt must be paid, and in some cases, the burden may fall on your beneficiaries. Careful planning can assure that this will not happen, as discussed in chapter 7.

CASE LAW OR COMMON LAW

Besides the written laws and regulations passed and published by federal, state, and local governments, each jurisdiction follows the "case law" or "common law" of certain higher courts. This type of law is also called "precedent." For example, a decision handed down by the U.S. Supreme Court sets a precedent that must be followed by all the other American courts; but a decision made by the Maryland Supreme Court only sets a "binding" precedent (that is, it must be followed) by the Maryland courts. The courts of other states may look to the Maryland decision for what is called "persuasive" authority—that is, for an idea on how to decide a similar issue their own higher courts have not yet ruled upon. But they may choose to take a different approach.

The court decisions that set binding precedent for a particular jurisdiction often change the way a statute works, or add to its requirements. If you are preparing your own will, you may follow the "letter of the law" as set out in your state's statutes to a "T" and still miss a vital step you must take to make one of the provisions effective, because that particular point is a matter of case law, not statutory law in your state. For example, in New Mexico, the case law requires that one who wishes to exclude a blood relative from inheriting must include certain language in her will if the exclusion is to be legally effective. This language is not set out in the probate statute—it has been added by the court-made common law or case law. This is one of the primary reasons it is essential to consult with professionals who, as a part of their job, stay abreast of these changes.

SHOULD I TRY TO AVOID PROBATE?

Until the mid-1960s, most people had only a simple will to address their estate planning needs—if they had thought about estate planning at all! As a result, most estates went through some type of probate procedure. In many jurisdictions, probate procedures were antiquated, unduly complex, and expensive. The late senator Robert F. Kennedy once referred to the probate system as "a political tollbooth extracting tribute from widows and orphans." Abuses of the probate system, including the exorbitant fees sometimes charged by unscrupulous lawyers, led to a public demand for a reform.

During the sixties, attempts to reform the probate system began to occur on several diverse fronts. The Uniform Probate Code, designed to streamline and simplify the process, was drafted by a group of lawyers and judges and adopted by the legislatures of many states. Other states, while not adopting the Uniform Probate Code, reworked their own laws to achieve the same effect.

Living trusts also came to the public's attention, in large part due to a financial planner named Norman F. Dacey. Dacey's specialty was introducing his clients to then-obscure estate planning tools, such as trust documents, to help them avoid probate. In 1964, following a complaint from the Connecticut Bar Association that accused him of practicing law without a license, Dacey was enjoined from continuing his estate-planning services. So in 1966 he wrote and published a book titled *How to Avoid Probate!* It rocketed to the number one spot on the *New York Times* best-seller list, bumping Masters & Johnson's *Human Sexual Response* to number two, and prompting Dacey to hastily disclaim charges that he had managed to make probate more interesting than sex.

The main thrust of his tome introduced readers to the concept that by placing property in trust, they could avoid the effort and expense of probate. The book contained forms the reader could tear out and complete to set up various types of trusts, purportedly without having to consult an attorney. Even today, *How to Avoid Probate!* continues to be a popular manual, and has been republished in several updated editions.

While Dacey's book tends to oversimplify the process—you already know my opinion of trying to complete your estate plan without competent legal counsel—it does provide a good overview of advantages and options available by using trusts as estate planning tools. Perhaps best of all, it made the public aware of an estate planning option that has saved many people a great deal of time and money.

Trusts are discussed in some detail in a later chapter, but living trusts are described briefly here as they relate to probate law. Property that is passed to your beneficiaries through a living trust does not have to go through the probate process. Establishing a living trust generally requires two steps: First, the trust documents establish the trust itself as a legal entity; name a trustee (the person who will manage and control the property held in trust; usually the individual who owns the property and establishes the trust); any cotrustees (such as a spouse); successor trustees (who will take over the trustee's duty if she becomes incapacitated or when she dies); and beneficiaries. Second, property must be transferred into the trust. When the maker of the trust (also called the "settlor" or "trustor") dies, the property automatically passes to the beneficiaries without requiring any court involvement, so there is no probate.

While probate can be an expensive and time-consuming process, avoiding probate is not always desirable. In some situations, it is the simplest and most economical way for assets to be transferred. Much depends on the size of your estate and the state in which you live. For a small estate that can be probated through the informal procedure, it may be less expensive and take less time to prepare a will and distribute the estate through the probate process than to do the work involved in creating a living trust and transferring assets into the trust. In some jurisdictions, however, probate may take as long as two years, while the property involved remains in limbo.

Also, in many states, the statutes set the probate fees, which may or may not ensure that the cost of the process is reasonable. For example, in California and some other states, probate fees are based upon a percentage of the estate's total value. This is determined according to fair market value, which could lead to an unfair result, for example, when real estate is involved. The court doesn't look at the equity in a piece of real estate but rather the property's entire value. Therefore, if the decedent owned a home worth $100,000 but owed $75,000 on an outstanding mortgage, the probate fee is still set based on the $100,000 value. Thus, if the probate fee is set as 5 percent of the value of the estate, this results in a fee of $5,000, even though there was only $25,000 equity in the home. In such a case, use of a living trust or other non-probate transfer tool would be well worth the extra time and cost of setting it up.

Whether you choose to have a will, a living trust, or both, realize that these are not necessarily the only tools you need to plan your estate. There are other essential considerations, and if these are neglected, the outcome can be heartbreaking for family members of the person who dies without having their affairs in order.

For example, in a case described by financial adviser Suze Orman in her book *The 9 Steps to Financial Freedom,* a married woman with two young children who had owned the family home since before her marriage in her own name, made a will, leaving everything to her husband, after she was diagnosed with breast cancer. Her health insurance covered most, but not all, of her medical treatment, and excluded the hospice care that would allow her to spend her final days at home after it became apparent that she would not recover. Her husband, who was self-employed, turned down work to help care for his wife, and used credit cards to pay for her hospice expenses.

After she died, her husband, who was already overwhelmed by the weight of his grief and the responsibility of raising their children alone, learned that in spite of the fact that his wife had a will, he faced enormous probate, attorneys, and credit-card debts that would almost certainly require him to sell the house.

This sad catastrophe could have been avoided in several ways. First, a more comprehensive health insurance plan, and/or life insurance, could have avoided or paid off the husband's debt for hospice care. Second, if the home had been held in joint tenancy, or transferred to a living trust, probate expenses would have been avoided. This family lived in California, where probate costs are often astronomical. State probate laws differ, but it is always a good idea to learn about your options to simplify property transfers and save money should your family face a similar situation.

ESTATE, INCOME, GIFT, AND OTHER TAX LAWS

It's been said that the only two certainties in life are death and taxes. When these topics intertwine, the complexity can be enough to give the most blasé tax accountant a headache.

Because the issue of taxation arises in conjunction with nearly every individual topic addressed in this book, rather than try to provide any kind of preliminary overview, it makes greater sense to discuss the impact of tax concerns in conjunction with each topic as it arises. But here are a few basic facts to keep in mind as you consider the estate planning issues important to your situation:

1. Federal estate taxes are only charged against estates with a total net value of $650,000 (in 1999). Estates with a lesser value are exempt from this tax. In 2000, the exempt amount goes up to $675,000; in 2002 to $700,000; in 2004 to $850,000; in 2005 to $950,000; and in 2006 to $1,000,000.
2. Benefits paid from life insurance *do* count in calculating your estate's total value. The beneficiary (for instance, your surviving spouse) won't have to pay income tax on life insurance benefits, but if your estate exceeds the exempt amount, estate taxes will be charged against the total, including life insurance.
3. Federal estate taxes are levied at *high* rates, up to 55 percent for the highest tax brackets. Be sure you know the total net value of your estate, so that if it is likely to be greater than the exempt amount, you can take steps to protect it. (Many people are surprised to learn the value

of their holdings, but when life insurance, real estate, and perhaps a small business are combined, what seems to be a modest estate can exceed the exempt figure.) Trusts and other plans to avoid or lower estate tax liability can be set up for relatively little time and cost, and are well worth the effort.

4. A living trust does *not* affect the value of your estate for purposes of calculating estate taxes. Other types of trusts can be established to help you avoid or ease the estate tax crunch, but simply placing your assets in a living trust, while it helps you avoid probate costs, has no effect on the value of your estate for calculating estate taxes.
5. Making gifts during your lifetime (inter vivos giving), within the amounts exempt from gift tax ($10,000 per year to each recipient at the present time) can be an effective way to avoid capital-gains tax and certain other tax bites. But if you make gifts greater than the exempt amount, their value—less any gift tax you paid—may be added to the total value of your estate for the purpose of calculating whether and how much estate tax your estate will owe.
6. The beneficiaries of your estate won't be required to pay federal income tax on what they inherit, but a number of states charge inheritance taxes. Some states' inheritance taxes are structured so that they only apply to estates that are subject to federal estate taxes and may be deducted from the federal taxes paid, so there is, in effect, no additional charge beyond the federal estate taxes; others' inheritance taxes differ and do amount to an additional tax burden.

These are some of the most basic and frequently misunderstood death-tax issues. *Many* others may arise, depending on your individual circumstances and estate plan, and these are discussed throughout the book. The good news is that for nearly every tax problem, there is some way to ease the burden.

"GRANNY GOES TO JAIL" LAW

As a part of their estate-planning efforts, many people begin giving away their property while they are still alive in order to lower the value of their estates at death for tax purposes, as well as to make them eligible for various government benefits, such as Medicare or Medicaid when they get older and may need health-care cost assistance.

On January 1, 1997, the U.S. Congress passed a law that made it a federal crime to "knowingly and willfully" dispose of assets for less than their fair-market value "in order for an individual to become eligible for medical assistance (such as nursing-home benefits), if disposing of the assets results in the imposition of a period of ineligibility for such assistance."

This controversial law, called the "Health Insurance Portability and Accountability Act of 1996," could reach inter vivos gifts, as well as assets transferred to a trust. The law provided that fines could be levied up to $25,000, along with prison terms of up to five years. Before the law was passed, transfers for such a purpose could have resulted in delayed eligibility but no charges of having committed a federal crime.

Additionally, under the 1996 law, criminal penalties applied only if a state first delayed Medicaid eligibility because of an asset transfer and the state found that the individual intentionally made an illegal transfer. The law included some exceptions for spouses and people with disabilities.

Not surprisingly, this law proved extremely unpopular, and senior's advocates immediately launched a campaign to have it repealed. The law's goal was to track down fraud and abuse, but the American Association of Retired Persons (AARP) objected to its broad applicability, which, it charged, could harm those who were trying to achieve legitimate estate-planning goals. The AARP and others supported a bill introduced by Congressman Steven Latourette to repeal the provision.

In August 1997, Congress agreed to repeal the law and instead passed a "jailing granny's lawyer" law, which made it a crime for anyone, including attorneys, for a fee, to knowingly and willfully counsel or assist a person to dispose of assets in order to become eligible for benefits "if the disposition of the assets results in the imposition of a period of ineligibility for such assistance . . ."

Again, it was no surprise when this law was challenged as unconstitutional. New York and Rhode Island had brought challenges to the "jailing granny's lawyer" law by November 1997. By the spring of 1998, U.S. Attorney General Janet Reno reported to

Congress that the Department of Justice would not defend the constitutionality of the law, Section 1128(B)(A)(6) of the Social Security Act. Reno stated that the counseling prohibition in the provision was plainly unconstitutional under the First Amendment and that the Department of Justice would not bring any criminal prosecutions under the current version of the section.

So where does all this legal wrangling leave the average American trying to use gifts as a part of his estate planning? Essentially, where they were before the law was enacted. This means, in most cases, that as long as at least thirty months have passed between the time a person transferred assets and applied for Medicaid, your eligibility for Medicaid—and the legality of the transfer—cannot be challenged (if less than thirty months have elapsed, Medicaid may place a lien on the home or other asset, but this is all that will happen). However, it seems likely that new laws aimed to stop fraudulent transfers of property in order to become eligible for government benefits—which may also affect legitimate gift-giving for estate planning purposes—may be enacted soon. Be sure you understand the current laws that could impact such gifts before you transfer your property.

■ Chapter 3

WILLS

A will is a traditional legal document in which the person making the will (the "testator") identifies those individuals or institutions he wishes to receive his property and possessions upon death. These individuals and institutions are usually referred to as beneficiaries, or, in some cases, devisees. In the interest of consistency, we will refer to anyone designated to receive property from someone else who has died—whether through a will, trust, or other instrument—as the beneficiary.

The will appoints a personal representative (PR), also called an executor or administrator in some states, who gathers and distributes property upon your death, pays the estate's bills, and takes care of other business. The PR may be an individual or an institution. Common choices for this executor role include a primary beneficiary under the will (such as an adult child), an attorney, or a financial institution that manages most of your assets. (The role and duties of the PR are discussed in more detail later in this chapter.)

WHAT DOES A WILL DO?

The will is the most basic estate planning device. Even those who plan to transfer most of their property through other estate planning methods, such as living trusts or property held in joint tenancy, generally need a will as well, for several reasons. First, a will serves as a backup device to transfer any property you may have overlooked, or property you unexpectedly acquire after your estate planning documents are set up, such as an inheritance or prize winnings. Lawyers who prepare living trusts almost always write this type of simple will (often called a "pourover will") in conjunction with setting up the trust. Also, a will is the only document you can use to name a personal guardian for your minor children. A will is also the best way to transfer certain types of property that are not convenient to transfer by other methods, such as some personally held bank accounts.

A will may be the only estate planning device necessary for those who simply do not need more complex methods and live in an area where probate is not a major ordeal (as discussed in the previous chapter). For example, a couple with a modest estate may already own their home in joint tenancy, so each spouse's interest in the property automatically passes to the other upon their death. A will that names a guardian for minor children and leaves property which is not valuable enough to be subject to estate or other death tax to their beneficiaries is probably all they really need for the moment.

Even so, a qualified attorney should review the couple's wills to be sure they meet the state's requirements for validity; that their gross assets, including life insurance, a small business, or a home that has sharply appreciated in value, do not bump the total value of the estates into the taxable range; and that the plan they have created does not invoke problems with other laws, such as community property of spousal allowances. It is important for people in this situation to review their estate planning occasionally as they get older and their assets, goals, and needs change.

The rights and requirements surrounding wills are determined by each state's legislature. In most, any person who has reached the age of majority and is of sound mind may make a will. "Sound mind" simply means that the person must understand what they are doing by executing a will. This is called "testamentary capacity." People are generally presumed to have this capacity unless someone proves otherwise. People may be unable to conduct their daily affairs, be undeniably eccentric, or mentally declining with age yet still remain competent. In legalese, so long as they know the extent of their estate, the natural object of their bounty, where they want their property to go, and understand that they are making a will, they are presumed to be in the requisite state of "sound mind."

"Natural objects of the testator's bounty" refers to family members and close friends. However, the law does not state or imply that these people should be the beneficiaries. It may require that relatives within this category be specifically excluded if they are not intended to inherit. With few exceptions, a person who makes a will may leave their estate to anyone they choose, including organizations or companies, as well as people. In most states, the only prohibited beneficiaries are animals, the father of an illegitimate child who has not acknowledged or provided for the child, or a potential beneficiary who intentionally kills the decedent.

Conditions may also be attached to bequests, for example, that an heirloom must not be sold or gifted to anyone outside the family, or that Peter will receive his inheritance only if he finishes college. Eccentric conditions have been enforced in the courts, and generally speaking, the only conditions that will not be enforced are those that are illegal (ten thousand dollars to Evelyn—but only if she kills Pablo), or are contrary to public policy (Festus must divorce Bethany before he may receive the deed to the home).

The requirements for execution of a valid will vary from state to state. In most, the will must be in writing and signed by the testator in the presence of one or more witnesses, who also sign the will in the presence of the testator and other witnesses. Some states require the signature on a will to be at the bottom; others do not specify where it is to be signed. Requirements for witnesses vary. Almost every state's law requires the witnesses to be "present." This sounds like a simple mandate but has led to a surprising amount of confusion and conflict in the courts. The traditional view, adopted by most states, is called the "line of sight" test. Under it, the presence requirement is met if the witnesses could have seen the required signing if they had looked—not that they actually watched the signing occur. A more modern view, adopted in a minority of jurisdictions, is the "conscious presence" test. This means that the witness was aware of what was happening and the act was within the purview of her five senses. Thus, under the conscious presence test, the witness could be in another room but heard the testator call out that he was signing and heard the pen scratching across the paper.

Many state statutes require witnesses to be "attesting witnesses," which means that they can generally attest to the testator's capacity to legally make a will. This means that if called to testify, they could state that to the best of their knowledge and belief, based on their observation of the testator while he was executing the will, there was no reason to suspect that he was anything less than competent. This does not require that they know the person well, only that they became vaguely familiar with the person's demeanor during the execution process.

Most states require "credible witnesses," which means that the individuals acting as witnesses are competent under the state's requirement to testify to the facts of the execution of the will, as well as to the mental capacity of the testator. Some states have specific age requirements, but most do not. Generally, anyone who could competently testify as a witness in court is considered to be competent to witness a will.

However, there is one important exception. A witness should be someone who does not have a "beneficial interest" in the will. Under a long tradition of common law, the witness cannot be a beneficiary. Many states have enacted statutes that authorize someone with an interest under the will to act as a witness without affecting the validity of the will, but if it is challenged, this can be raised as evidence that the witness was not impartial. It is best to use witnesses who are completely disconnected from the will. Often, secretaries or other employees of the attorney who prepares the will act as witnesses.

Sometimes, after a will is executed, the need to take another step to prove that it is valid arises. A testator and witness may "self-prove" a will by acknowledging before an officer of the state, such as a notary public, that they witnessed and signed the document according to all the requirements of the applicable law.

Testamentary Trusts

Although trusts are discussed in greater detail in chapter 4, one special kind of trust must be mentioned here. A testamentary trust is one that is contained within a will. It takes effect to manage and distribute the property contained in the trust only when the testator dies. Some people, for example, establish in their will a trust for a minor child and name a trustee to manage the money until the child reaches a certain age, at which time the proceeds are distributed.

Testamentary trusts can be a convenient way to consolidate such goals in a single document but should be handled with skill and care, because of the tax implications and other potential consequences. Also, a testamentary trust does not serve the purpose of avoiding the time and cost of probate, as a living trust does, because it is a part of the will and must therefore pass through the probate process. A living trust can accomplish the same goals as a testamentary trust without requiring probate.

Both wills and living trusts can include and incorporate other trusts, often called "subtrusts." These may include bypass trusts, special trusts for children, or a trust set up to provide care for aging parents. A living trust can do everything a will can except appoint a guardian for children. The key is to make sure, whether you have a will, a living trust, or both, that you have what is adequate to cover all your needs in the state where you live.

Trusts, whether contained in a separate will or living trust, or created on their own, are varied in what they may achieve. The key is to work with a competent professional or set of professionals to be sure that any trust you create is right for you, and that you understand all of the consequences of creating the trust. For example, trusts that contain powers of appointment can be general or specific, and they can have tax consequences. A trust is a contract, and it can be done in many ways, with innumerable variations.

Codicils

One who wishes to change a will does not necessarily have to create an entirely new document. A "codicil" is an addition to or modification of an existing will. Because it performs the same function as a will, however, a codicil must be executed with the same formalities, including being written, dated, bearing the testator's signature, and the signature of witnesses. The codicil should also specify what sections of the will remain in effect. Some states add other requirements, such as notarization. A codicil can also correct defects that may make a will invalid. This is called "republication by codicil."

Never try to make changes in a will by simply crossing things out and rewriting words or sentences. If a person attempts to alter a will without formally executing a new one, or a codicil, the change is usually considered invalid. However, the will itself remains valid and may be offered for probate as it was originally written. Of course, wills sometimes are altered before they are executed. If a will is offered for probate and on the face of the document it appears that certain things have been changed, the proponent—the person offering the will for probate—has the burden of proving that the alterations were made before the will was executed.

A codicil can be a convenient way to make small changes to a complex will without having to redo the entire document. However, if you try to use a codicil to make major changes, this can lead to confusion. Also, a will with several codicils attached may become cumbersome or confusing. Most attorneys advise that the entire will be redone if more than two or three codicils are required.

Whenever you make a new will, it is generally best to destroy all copies of old wills unless you are concerned that your new will may be contested. If this is the case, be sure to write "REVOKED" in large letters across the first page of the will (not in the margin). Old wills that reflect an ongoing, similar intent may be admitted in a will contest as evidence of how you wanted your estate to be distributed. For example, if a disinherited relative claims that your last will was the product of the undue influence of another relative and therefore does not reflect your "true" aim of dividing your estate equally among your relatives, old wills showing that you never had such an intent can help quash the challenger's argument.

Personal Property and Small Bequests

When preparing their estates, many people wish to designate a number of friends or family members who will receive small gifts of property such as jewelry or family heirlooms, that have sentimental value. Yet, a long list of bequests can add complexity to a will, particularly if the maker changes his mind several times about who is to receive what.

In most states, a list of small bequests, called a "tangible personal property list," can be handwritten and signed by the maker, and does not have to be a part of the will or trust document. The will or trust agreement contains a simple clause instructing the personal representative or trustee to refer to the tangible personal property list to make the required distributions. It is much easier to change this list than it is to make an entirely new will or trust. Be sure to check with your attorney if you wish to use a tangible personal property list, since some states do not allow them.

Holographic Wills

A "holographic will" is a will that is in the testator's handwriting. Generally, no part of it may be typed or printed. The paper on which the will is written must have no other writing on it. In some states, holographic wills need not meet the same formalities of execution as standard wills, but in many states the same requirements apply to both types of wills. In other states, it is presumed that holographic wills are not witnessed, and having such a will signed by witnesses will actually make it null and void. In a few states, holographic wills are no longer recognized as valid under any circumstances.

Holographic wills are uncommon today, but they still appear occasionally, usually prepared long ago by an older person who did not have access to legal assistance. Holographic wills are inevitably problematic for the courts, and often lead to litigation when someone challenges their validity. The best advice regarding holographic wills is to have them redone according to current state legal requirements.

Oral or Videotaped Wills

Most states do not permit oral wills, although a few recognize their validity under specific circumstances (for example, a soldier who is about to die on the battlefield). None allow videotaped wills, despite the popularity of such wills for dramatic effect on television. A person may prepare a videotape reading of his will, but the will itself must be a written document in line with state law. However, such a videotape, in addition to the dramatic possibilities, may be admissible as evidence of competency and intent should the will be challenged and end up in litigation, as discussed below.

Moving

What happens when a person makes a will in one state or country and then moves to another? Usually, a will validly executed in another jurisdiction according to its laws will be admitted into probate and enforced in the state where the testator was domiciled when she died. But it may be a good idea to make a new will after a move for several reasons. It is more convenient for those involved in the probate if a will is in line with the law of the state where the decedent lived at the time of death. Also, if you move, you should include in your will any property you sold or purchased during the course of your move.

You may also need to determine whether the move changed your situation to the extent that a different type of estate planning might now be preferable. For example, if you still own the home where you lived in another state and now use it as rental property, it might be wise to consider putting it into some type of trust arrangement to avoid multistate probates and other potential problems.

Also, remember that the states vary enormously in the speed and expense of their probate procedures. If, for instance, you live in Santa Fe, your attorney may have advised you that your will is perfectly adequate because your estate is not complex and probate procedures are fast and inexpensive in New Mexico. If you move to Los Angeles, the picture changes considerably. California's probate process is much slower, and the legally set probate fees may result in tremendous cost to your estate. Thus, by virtue of the move alone, it may be well worth your while to place your property in a living trust instead of passing it through a will.

ADVANCES AGAINST INHERITANCE AND CONTRACTS TO BEQUEATH

Occasionally, a person may wish to give one of their beneficiaries, usually a child, an advance against money they would otherwise inherit. For example, the parents of several children may choose to pay medical school tuition for their daughter who aspires to be a doctor, while holding the rest of their estate for their other children who do not have such an immediate need for money. In fairness to all, the parents may wish to treat this gift as an advance against inheritance rather than as an outright gift.

Conversely, people occasionally wish to wait to bestow a gift on someone until after she has performed a certain duty or fulfilled a set condition, such as providing care for the person for the remaining years of his life. In this case, he may enter into a contract in which he promises to provide for this person through a will or trust after his death, in exchange for services or other promises fulfilled while he is alive.

In the former case, it is generally preferable, but not necessary, to have the advance against inheritance designated as such in a written agreement. Disputes often erupt after a person dies. For example, the child who received medical school tuition insists that it was an outright gift, whereas her siblings claim that it was an advance against inheritance. Her parent intended but did not clearly express a desire to reduce that child's share of the estate by a proportionate amount.

Of course, good estate planning avoids such disputes by clearly stating all of the individual's relevant intentions. It is often beneficial, however, if you suspect that a question may arise after your death to state your intentions in more than one way—and in more than one written document. (This is discussed in more detail later in this chapter in relation to how to prevent will contests.) Some states have specific laws that require such agreements to be in writing if they are to have any legal effect.

In the case of a contract to inherit, again, this generally won't be a problem even if a separate contract were never created, as long as the will or trust is clear as to the testator's intent. However, the courts have seen more than their share of battles over a supposed contract to inherit when the estate plan was not clear, or when an elderly person was involved and someone raised a question of duress, undue influence, or incompetence.

For this reason, as well as many others, people occasionally provide brief explanations in their wills or accompanying estate-planning documents that note why they chose to make certain gifts or, for example, distributed their estate unequally among their children. Such explanations are generally short, a sentence or two or a paragraph. For example, "To my son Jasper Smith the sum of $10,000. I leave Jasper a smaller amount than his brother and sister because I paid $20,000 for Jasper's medical school tuition, and paid no college tuition for David or Sarah." These explanations may also be included in a separate document, such as a simple letter or similar communication referenced in the will, so that this information remains private. When a will is filed with the probate court, it becomes a public document, so that anyone who is interested can read it.

COMMON PROBLEMS WITH WILLS

Unfortunately, problems with wills, or challenges to their validity, are not a rare occurrence in probate courts. Sometimes the problems are essentially clerical. For example, a question of "integration" may arise when there is uncertainty as to which papers and terms were intended to be a part of a will at the time it was executed. In most cases, a will's pages are stapled together or numbered, so it is easy to tell by the flow of language which pages are meant to go together. However, questions of integration sometimes require the "proponent" (the person filing the will for probate) to prove that the will being offered is actually the will the testator intended to make—again, the court's primary job is to carry out the testator's intention.

Sometimes a will incorporates other documents or papers by reference. If the paper or a previous version of it was in existence when the will was executed, it can be identified as the paper referred to in the will. If language indicates that the paper is meant to be incorporated, most states consider these documents to be a part of the will, even though they were not executed with the same testamentary formalities. For example, as discussed, some people prepare an informal list of personal possessions they want distributed to specific individuals, and they incorporate this list by reference into the will.

As described in the introduction, some trusts include a "power of appointment," which requires the trust's maker to designate the ultimate beneficiaries of the trust assets in his will. While this arrangement may be convenient under some circumstances, it tends to be unwieldy for many people, and, as we've shown, can lead to disaster if the maker forgets or does not realize that he must make this designation in his will. This type of trust must be handled carefully.

Far more common than the above scenarios is the problem of an ambiguous will. The fundamental rule in the construction of wills is the same as it is for contracts: The court is supposed to determine the testator's intention from the whole instrument (sometimes called "the four corners of the document")—and nothing else. If a will is not ambiguous, additional evidence to explain its terms is usually inadmissible under the rules of evidence. However, if the court finds that a will is so unclear that the judge cannot determine what the testator wanted to have done with her estate, other evidence may be considered in order to show the testator's circumstances at the time she made her will.

Courts are guided in this task by various rules of construction, which are intended to help them discover the testator's intent. The first rule comes from the idea that a person who makes a will does not wish to die intestate, so whenever possible, the will must be construed by the court so as to avoid this outcome. However, a second rule states that a construction is favored that most closely conforms to the laws of descent and distribution, as set forth in the intestate statutes.

Courts often encounter three distinct types of mistakes in wills. The first is called "mistake in the inducement," which means that the testator was mistaken about a fact that led him to dispose of property in a way he would not have chosen if he had known the true facts. Most courts won't try to reform a will because of a mistake in the inducement. The second type of mistake is called a "mistake in the factum," which relates to the nature or contents of the document itself. For example, it is sometimes claimed that the testator signed the will believing it was, in fact, a different document than the one she signed. This commonly occurs when a husband and wife execute wills together and inadvertently sign the will of the other person. Most courts deny probate of a will under these circumstances.

However, a second type of mistake in the factum occurs when a paragraph in the will is erroneously included or omitted. In this case, most courts simply deny probate to that portion of the will. The wrongfully included clause is deleted. If the error is in an omission, the court usually probates the will according to its meaning without the omitted portion, unless that portion is so vital to the total testamentary plan that the court determines there was a serious lack of testamentary intent. Some wills contain a clause—like a standard clause included in many contracts—providing that if one portion of the will is invalid or unenforceable for some reason, it will not affect the rest of the will's validity.

The third type of mistake is called "mistake in the description," which means a mistake exists in the will itself, such as an address or other description of real estate. A court usually won't reform a will when it appears this type of mistake has occurred.

Sometimes problems arise when a person named as a beneficiary in a will dies before the testator does, and the will was never amended to name a new beneficiary. Confusion may also arise when a charitable organization is named to receive a bequest, and by the time of the testator's death, the charity has disbanded.

Therefore, people often name alternate beneficiaries or otherwise state in their will what should happen if a named beneficiary dies first. This may include naming a different person, or simply providing that the bequest becomes a part of the residual estate. You should also name an alternate residuary beneficiary.

Your beneficiaries should be plainly identified by full name and address in your will or trust. If you wish to leave a portion of your estate to an organization, occasionally check to be sure that the name you have designated in your will or other estate planning documents is still accurate. It is also helpful to identify such organizations by address and brief description, so that if you miss out on a name change, the charity can still be identified.

It may also be important to clearly identify any person who is a close relative whom you wish to disinherit. Different states have different legal requirements to disinherit those who might otherwise have a claim to your estate, such as a child. States do not require that you leave even a small bequest to a person you choose to disinherit. In some areas, it was once common to leave a small sum, such as one dollar, to such a person. Today, however, this only adds to the work of the personal representative, who must track down all of the named beneficiaries and deal with each bequest.

EXECUTORS, ADMINISTRATORS, PERSONAL REPRESENTATIVES, AND TRUSTEES

When the time comes to settle your estate, someone has to handle a broad range of chores and duties to accomplish all the things that are practically and legally required. If you have a will, this person (or in some cases, an institution such as a bank or law firm) is called the personal representative, executor, or administrator, depending on the state (collectively referred to here as the "PR").

If your assets are held in trust, these duties will be performed by the "successor trustee." (For those with both a will and a trust, the PR and successor trustee are often the same person.) Often, the trust's settlor acts as the trustee for as long as he is capable.

This makes sense, since most people want to manage and distribute their own assets as long as they are able. In this situation, the trust always names a successor trustee to take over in this role after the settlor's death or incapacity.

After a person dies, the PR or successor trustee serves almost identical functions, with the exception being that the trustee isn't required to follow the same court-supervised probate procedures as the PR. They are responsible for ensuring that the applicable legal requirements of settling the estate, and the decedent's wishes as expressed in the will or trust, are carried out. Both the PR and trustee have similar fiduciary responsibilities; that is, they have a legally heightened duty to act solely for the benefit of the beneficiaries named in the will or trust.

People often choose a spouse, adult child, relative, close friend, business associate, attorney, or institution such as a bank to act as PR or trustee. In choosing someone to fill this role, keep in mind that you should select one who is organized, responsible, and able to maintain books and records. For a larger estate or one with substantial investments, the executor or trustee should be someone with experience in business, finance, and/or investments.

Your PR or trustee is legally entitled to be paid a fee for his services, according to most state's statutes. Most institutions or professionals charge and accept a fee. This can be a fair trade-off for handling all the details and being certain that a large or complex estate is handled properly. However, if you name an individual who is also a beneficiary of your estate, he may decline the fee for two reasons: First, the fee is paid out of the estate, so if the person is the primary beneficiary, taking the fee would simply amount to moving funds that he would receive anyway. Second, the PR's fee is considered income and is subject to taxation, while money received as an inheritance is not subject to federal income tax (although it may be subject to inheritance tax in some states, as discussed later). Thus, in many cases, it is to the PR's advantage to decline the fee.

Those who do not have relatives or close friends whom they trust to adequately take care of their estate—and be comfortable in the role—may need to choose a professional or institution as personal representative or trustee. It is also advisable to name several alternates. Many people name a series of alternates to serve as personal representative or trustee. It is a good idea to select an institution as the last alternate. In many cases, by the time a person dies, everyone who was named as representative has predeceased him. With an institution such as a bank, it is likely that it or some successor institution will always be there.

If you create a living trust in which a professional individual (such as an attorney) or institution serves as trustee, you usually have to pay that person or business an annual fee. The amount charged by various trustees depends on a variety of factors, including their responsibilities, such as managing investments. Expect to pay additional charges if accounting, tax, or other advice is to be provided. Many people, especially those with more complex assets, find it helpful to shop around before making a final choice.

PR or Trustee's Duties

Your PR or trustee is responsible for wrapping up the details of your estate, including transferring titles and distributing property, paying creditors, collecting debts owed to the estate, and paying any taxes that are due. If anyone challenges the will or trust, he is also responsible for defending it.

Your PR should be someone who is willing, able, and qualified to perform the required duties. The complexity of these tasks naturally depends on your estate, but for even a simple estate, an individual PR usually must seek the assistance of one or more professionals to be sure the required duties are accomplished.

Your PR should be somewhat familiar with what you own, and should know where you keep your will, trust documents, pension and retirement papers, credit accounts, insurance policies, burial instructions, deeds, titles to vehicles, and other important records. You may wish to provide your PR with copies of these documents, as well as lists of relatives, other beneficiaries, and anyone else who needs to be informed when you die. She also needs to know about any bank accounts and safe-deposit boxes you may own, real estate, stocks and the broker who handles your investments, any safe-deposit or strongbox with combination or key location, and other important personal property and papers. Provide instructions on any special issues that could be hard to locate or easy to overlook, such as who is to care for pets and livestock, or important records stored on your computer or disks, and how to access these materials. If you prepared some form of a "panic book," "hurricane box," or other way to put your essential records and information in one place, as discussed in chapter 1, simply copying these materials for your PR or trustee works well.

If you do not have everything in one place, organizing these materials may seem like an overwhelming task, but it can provide you peace of mind both now and in the future, as well as cut down on the cost and effort required to settle your estate. As mentioned, if your records are in such disarray or you feel so overwhelmed that you simply cannot face this task, you might consider calling a professional organizer to assist you. These pros can help you develop a system that works for you, and structure a realistic plan to get the job done. They often provide their services for a surprisingly reasonable cost. For referrals to organizers in your area, check the yellow pages of your local telephone directory, or call the National Association of Professional Organizers (see Appendix).

The essential duties of your PR include locating your will and other estate documents; hiring an attorney and/or accountant to assist with probate, tax, and other legal requirements of closing the estate; preparing, signing, and submitting all the required court papers and tax forms; having mail forwarded to the personal representative; rounding up assets and completing a list of the assets and beneficiaries, then distributing them to the beneficiaries; listing and paying debts of the estate; and keeping an accounting of the estate's expenses and income.

The tax-related duties are probably the trickiest of these tasks, depending upon the estate. Whether or not your estate will owe taxes, your personal representative or trustee may be required to file a fiduciary income-tax return, Form 1041. The PR or trustee must file the decedent's federal and state income-tax forms, and a tax number must be obtained for the estate by use of IRS Form SS-4 or by requesting a number by calling (512) 462-7843. IRS Form 1041 must be filed if the estate assets will earn more than $600 gross income in a year. Probate attorneys and accountants are familiar with the steps that must be taken for each estate.

WILL CONTESTS AND HOW TO AVOID THEM

Will contests are among the ugliest, saddest, most emotionally and financially draining forms of litigation. If you have the slightest inkling that someone may be unhappy enough about the way you have set up your estate plan to challenge it after your death, it is well worth it to invest the time and money in a little legal overkill to be as certain as possible that this won't happen.

Of course, other forms of property transfer can be challenged as well, but it is the humble will that is most susceptible to attack. Trusts are not immune from challenge, but they tend to be viewed in a different light than wills, and are typically attacked less often. Generally speaking, anytime a will, trust, or other estate-planning tool is challenged, the same basic principles apply.

Will contests occur most often between siblings, or a child of the deceased and someone else who received property under the will. They can also arise under truly bizarre circumstances, when no one would suspect this could happen, as the story in the introduction illustrates.

Probate litigation is not confined to cases involving large estates. Sometimes, relatively small items of property are involved—a family heirloom, a modest home, a vehicle. When rivalries have smoldered between siblings for years, they often erupt in the emotionally charged atmosphere that surrounds a parent's death. This leads to lawsuits that accomplish nothing more than to escalate bad feelings and diminish or destroy the value of the property at issue.

While there are a few cases in which contesting a will is a valid undertaking—for example, when an incapacitated person was plainly bullied into signing a will that did not reflect her wishes—these lawsuits are, generally speaking, best avoided at nearly any cost.

The most effective way to prevent a contest over your estate is, of course, to make certain before your death that your goals and intentions are clearly spelled out and that you have taken all the required steps to see that they are accomplished. One important part of this process is the appointment of a trusted guardian to represent your interests in case you become incapacitated, as discussed later in the book.

Also, if you want to make a gift that could be considered unusual, take special precautions to be sure that your intentions are clear and well established. For example, a few years ago the national news reported that an elderly multimillionaire left the bulk of his estate to a waitress who had been especially kind and attentive to him on his daily visits to a neighborhood coffee shop. Fortunately, no one challenged the gift, and the young woman received the money her friend had wished her to have. But this is exactly the type of situation in which a greedy, disinherited relative often tries to contest the will.

If you choose not to leave property to one of your children or someone else who might be considered a "natural object of the testator's bounty," be sure that your intention to disinherit is stated in your will, as discussed above. Many people cite the reason for excluding this individual. It may be that you simply wish to provide for someone with whom you are closer, or who has a greater need for the property. This is a common clause that is included for clarity, and is, in fact, required in some states to effectively exclude a blood relative. No one should suffer hurt feelings as a result of such a clause, unless they are being disinherited from a bequest they expected. It is always best to discuss your intentions with family members, so that they understand your wishes.

Will contests are usually brought on grounds of incapacity, undue influence, duress, or fraud (or some combination of these factors). Other legal theories are available, but these are most frequently raised. The burden of proof is on the person challenging the will and claiming that the maker was unfairly persuaded to make a will that did not reflect his true intentions.

This can be a heavy burden. However, courts are often called upon to weigh scanty and conflicting evidence on both sides. This is why it is so important to try to create adequate evidence of your competence and desires for your estate while you are still alive and well.

Incapacity

Incapacity and undue influence are often raised together. "Incapacity" refers to someone who lacks the "sound mind" or "testamentary capacity" required to know what he is doing by making a will, who natural objects of his affections (i.e., friends and family) are, and state his wishes about how his estate should be distributed after his death. People who have become incapacitated are often vulnerable to the "undue influence" of others, who take advantage of them.

Advanced age is one component of evidence often introduced in an attempt by a will challenger to prove undue influence or incapacity. Age alone is not supposed to be considered an indication of diminished capacity or susceptibility to influence, but, in fact, the issue often arises, as illustrated by the story in the introduction. Therefore, if you are creating or revising your estate plan during your senior years, and fear that someone may challenge it, it is important to be sure that evidence of your competence and free expression of your desires will be available after your death.

Duress

When someone uses threats or intimidation to force another person to behave in a certain way, that individual is said to be "acting under duress." This is not a common charge in will contests, but it does happen. For example, cases have been brought to court in which someone charged that a person who was caring for an aged relative threatened to withhold care or harm him if he did not change his will to make the caretaker a beneficiary. Anytime threats are used to force someone to do something they would not otherwise do, an issue of duress arises.

Undue Influence

Undue influence is similar to duress but does not necessarily involve such a sinister use of direct threats or intimidation. In fact, it may arise when someone is accused of ingratiating themselves with another through insincere kindness, then manipulating her into changing her will in the person's favor. The test for undue influence asks whether the testator was susceptible to the person's influence, whether this person had the opportunity to exert undue influence, whether he had a motive to influence the testator, and if the will was a product of these factors.

Courts analyzing a charge of undue influence look at whether a "confidential relationship" existed between the third party and the testator. A confidential relationship refers to one in which the circumstances indicate that the testator would place trust and confidence in the other person, for example, an adult child taking care of an elderly parent. Under the law in many states, a confidential relationship combined with other suspicious circumstances is enough to raise the presumption of undue influence. However, unless the person challenging the will can prove that the testator's free will was impaired or destroyed by this influence, the will cannot be set aside on grounds of undue influence.

Fraud

Fraud occurs when a testator makes a will that he would not have otherwise made, as a result of willful, false statements made by another. These statements must have been made in order to convince the testator to execute the will, or induce him to include certain provisions. Those seeking to prove fraud must establish that "but for" the false statements, the will or bequest would not have been made.

Sometimes two or more of these problems may arise in the same situation. For example, Molly, a woman in her eighties, has suffered steadily declining health over the past few years. She has two children, Joe (who lives with her and provides some care when she is ill) and Nancy (who lives with her own family in a distant city). Molly's will leaves her property to Joe and Nancy in equal shares, but Joe wants Molly to leave him everything. So he tries to convince Molly that Nancy no longer cares for her (when he, in fact, intercepts Nancy's weekly telephone calls and always tells her Molly is out or asleep); he falsely tells his mother that Nancy's husband makes so much money that the family doesn't need to inherit anything and persuades her that Nancy has developed a drinking problem and would squander anything she received on booze (another lie). After months of campaigning along these lines, Joe convinces Molly to change her will to leave her entire estate to him. Under these circumstances, Nancy could challenge the will based upon undue influence and fraud.

When the individual contesting a will succeeds in proving that it resulted from duress, fraud, or undue influence, the court must set the will aside, even if intestacy results. As shown in our example in the introduction, this is precisely what some contestants wish to achieve. Sometimes, only a portion of the will is affected by proof of fraud or undue influence. In that case, gifts and bequests that were included in other areas of the will can still pass through probate to the intended recipients. However, if there is a residuary clause, those bequests procured by fraud or undue influence may fall into the residual estate instead of passing into intestacy.

Evidence in Will Contests

The law's willingness to set aside a will when someone proves that it was a product of fraud, duress, or undue influence is based on the idea that if someone is induced to make a will that does not reflect his true intentions, then the court should not enforce it but should instead try to determine what the person really wanted. While a will that is clear and presumed valid will be enforced as written under most circumstances, if someone challenges its meaning or raises an issue that suggests it may have been the product of fraud, duress, or undue influence, the court can consider other evidence. Such evidence may include letters, other written documents, and the testimony of people who knew the deceased.

As with fraud, proving undue influence does not require direct evidence, since the influence is usually exerted in private. Circumstantial evidence may be all that is needed. Undue influence can arise anytime someone with power over the testator misuses it to cause her to make a will different from the one she would have made without this influence.

Under any of these theories, the person challenging the will must prove that the testator's free agency was effectively destroyed. It must be shown that the will reflects the wishes of another person rather than the wishes of the testator. This is usually a difficult matter to prove, but attempts arise with amazing frequency.

Practical Steps to Avoid Estate Battles

Albuquerque attorney Thomas J. Horne has represented clients in several cases in which wills were challenged. All were unpleasant. "It is far better to avoid this kind of problem in advance if at all possible," he comments.

In addition to insisting that the professionals you work with explain each and every component of your estate plan so that you understand it thoroughly, Horne advises that you write your own explanation of what you want to accomplish, and what you want done, in a letter. "Send copies of it to friends, family members, trustees, lawyers, and others, such as banks who hold your assets. This reaffirms your intentions in case a question arises later, or someone second-guesses what you were trying to accomplish, or a mistake shows up in a document," he explains.

Horne also points out that having property spread around different jurisdictions can add complexity. "If possible, it is better to have your assets in the same jurisdiction, where you are domiciled," he explains. "For example, if you have funds in trust in an out-of-state bank, this risks complications should any questions arise when your estate is being administered." Real estate can be especially difficult, since real property must be probated in the state where it is located. This is one reason many people transfer such property into living trusts, as discussed in greater depth later.

If you fear that a relative or someone else you've excluded from your will may try to make trouble for other beneficiaries after your death, there are several steps to take to minimize the chances of this occurring. As many people as possible should know about your estate-distribution plans at the time you set them up. If possible, make sure that in addition to your attorney and other advisers who help you plan your estate, at least five other people are well aware of your intentions. They may include trusted friends and family members, professional colleagues, or other individuals who know you and could testify that you were competent at the time you set up your estate plan, and that you knew and expressed to them your clear intentions at or after that time. Include several people who are not directly connected as beneficiaries or otherwise with your will or estate plan. If the situation arises, such people can provide neutral, disinterested testimony.

There are several ways this step may be taken. First, you may wish to write a letter to these individuals, and follow it up with a visit or phone call. It is important that you do so *after* you have made your estate plan, because if a real battle ensues, these people must testify that you were lucid, competent, and understood what you were doing both at and after the time you set up your estate plan.

Second, make good use of the people who witness the execution of your will and other pertinent documents. Often, witnessing is treated as a mere formality, with office personnel and others you may not know being called in to serve as witnesses. Generally, there is nothing wrong with this, since the witnesses' main purpose is to attest to the fact that the document's maker was indeed the person who signed the document. However, if you suspect that your estate plan may be challenged, the witnesses may be called on to testify as to their impressions of your mental state at the time you made the documents, as well as your general degree of competence, as far as they were aware of it. Someone who knows you fairly well may be a far more effective witness if problems occur later. The actual witnessing process generally does not take much time, so you may wish to ask a friend or colleague to accompany you when you execute your will and other documents. Check with your attorney to ensure that the people you have chosen as witnesses meet the requirements of your state's witness statute; generally, that they are the age of majority and are themselves legally competent.

Third, to take the process a step further, some attorneys advise including all the beneficiaries—or as many as possible—in the process of setting up and executing documents. If all parties are present when these arrangements are made, there is less chance that someone will later complain of confusion, unfairness, or undue influence. Any mistakes in the documents are more likely to be discovered at a time when they are easiest to correct. Horne advises following this procedure and then recording all of the powers of attorney and pertinent documents with the court immediately after they are executed.

Of course, such a step may not be appropriate or possible in all circumstances, as when the beneficiaries are widely scattered, or when the person setting up the estate plan wishes to keep her intentions confidential. In such a case, the inclusion in the process of neutral parties to review the documents, discuss the intent, and witness the proceedings can make up for the absent beneficiaries.

No states yet recognize the validity of "video wills" as a substitution for the traditional written documents. But a videotape can be powerful evidence to support these documents in stating your intentions and making them clear. If you make the videotape at the same time you set up your will and other estate planning documents, it can demonstrate your ability to state your wishes in a lucid manner and can also be powerful evidence that you were competent at the legally important point in time.

Today, it is easy and inexpensive to have a videotape made in which you state what you intend to accomplish with your estate plan. You might include statements on things you want to avoid, such as bickering between your children, and perhaps read your will or trust documents aloud to reaffirm that these documents reflect your intentions.

"No-Contest" Clauses

Many wills contain clauses stating that if anyone challenges the will, they shall receive nothing. These are seldom useful, because if a will is challenged as the product of fraud, duress, or undue influence, the entire document is usually (although not always) set aside if the charge is proven.

While "no-contest" clauses may carry relatively little weight from a legal standpoint, when a will is challenged, they may have the practical effect of preventing a challenge in the first place. For example, Mary's estate was distributed in a fairly equal manner among her six children. However, because the assets were not equivalent in their nature, since some of the children received cash and others received goods, one daughter, Carol, felt that she was not being treated fairly. She threatened to contest the will, until her brothers and sisters pointed out the no-contest clause, which convinced her that her case would be more difficult to win, and, more importantly, that her mother had expressed a strong desire that her children share the estate and not bicker about it. In the end, Carol accepted her share and made peace with her siblings.

What to Do If You Must Fight an Estate Battle

Wars over estates sometimes erupt, no matter how carefully it was planned. In some cases, litigation may be required, as discussed above, to bring about the true wishes of a testator who was victimized by another. If you are drawn into a battle involving an estate, those who have endured this joyless process can offer advice on how to make it as painless as possible.

"First, try your best to reach a settlement with the other party or parties as early in the case as possible," advises attorney Horne, who has seen firsthand the damage, both financially and emotionally, that can be wrought by a drawn-out will contest. "Try to get the others to agree to mediation or some other form of alternative dispute resolution, or urge your lawyers to try to reach a settlement agreement with the other attorneys as early as possible. Remember, settlement is a good thing. It preserves the assets of the estate, which can be quickly depleted when litigation drags on."

Horne advises individuals to choose carefully the lawyer who will represent them in a will contest. "A probate attorney who is not also a litigator may not be aware of all the available remedies, such as demanding a jury," he explains. "Likewise, probate is a specialized area of law that in many cases does not lend itself well to the rules of litigation. Ideally, you should choose a lawyer who is skilled at both probate matters and litigation, or a team that combines a litigator and probate attorney who work well together. Make sure the litigator understands the probate system, and the probate attorney is well versed in litigation."

Horne urges clients who are involved in estate litigation to remain closely attuned to what is happening throughout the case, and to monitor how the lawyers perform on their behalf. "Again, it is best to push for an early settlement if possible," he states. "The attorney should take depositions and do other discovery work early in the case, before the animosity builds. Sometimes lawyers get caught up in the battle, and make personal attacks on the opposing lawyers. This always works to the client's detriment. Anything in a case that escalates hostility is not in your best interests."

Horne acknowledges that various aspects of the law governing estates may not be clear, especially in the context of litigation. "As I once heard a judge say, 'When all else fails, read the law,'" he remarks. "It is important to research how the law in your state has been applied in similar situations. When the law is not clearly established on a particular point, or the attorney is unsure of how best to proceed, he can request instructions from the judge. This can be a good litigation strategy to move things along."

When probate litigation is not concluded as rapidly as possible, Horne says, the entire reason the case was brought may become moot. "I have seen legal fees consume more than half of a million-dollar estate when someone decided to contest a will," he recalls.

In most states, the statute that covers the formal probate procedure also governs will contests. However, like any courtroom proceeding, will contests are subject to the rules and laws that govern civil litigation in general. Thus, they are subject to many rules and requirements that add to the complicated nature of what is already bound to be a difficult lawsuit.

Consider Alternative Dispute Resolution

As attorney Horne noted above, estate contests can sometimes be settled through mediation, arbitration, or other forms of alternative dispute resolution. In this process, a case that would otherwise go to court is resolved in a more informal setting.

Mediation is a process in which the people involved in the dispute work with a neutral third party, the mediator, to try to reach an agreement that all can accept. Arbitration involves a similar process but is conducted in a somewhat more formal setting, one more like a court hearing, with the arbitrator or panel of arbitrators making the final decision on how the dispute will be resolved. Mediators and arbitrators often come from the ranks of retired judges, attorneys, psychologists, and trained community volunteers. To find a qualified mediator or arbitrator, the same steps apply as in locating other competent professionals. Begin with referrals from friends and colleagues. Or, seek referrals from professional organizations or community groups. Mediation is frequently used in settling divorce and other family law cases, so a family lawyer or family court may also be able to provide recommendations.

■ Chapter 4

Other Components of a Complete Estate Plan

Life and Death Planning

Many people have strong preferences about what they do or do not want to happen to them if they should become unable to care for themselves and handle their own business affairs. They also want to choose what shall be done with regard to their body and any memorial service. Today, people commonly execute legal documents that state these wishes and how they will be carried out, when they prepare their estate plan.

While none of us wants to think that we will ever be unable to direct our own lives, it is wise to have a plan in place. Perhaps the only thing worse than needing to use these tools is needing them and not having them. Preparing these documents is usually an easy, inexpensive process that many attorneys offer as part of a package of estate planning services.

The devices used to accomplish these goals may include living wills, directives to physicians, durable powers of attorney, funeral preplanning documents, and organ-donation directives. These documents, sometimes collectively referred to as "advance directives," set forth your wishes regarding medical treatment, and direct your doctors and family members to act accordingly if you are unable to state your wishes because you're incapacitated. They also appoint someone to make decisions if you cannot, and may appoint the same or another person to act upon your behalf in conducting business and personal affairs.

Advance directives may be temporary or permanent, and limited or unlimited in the powers they grant. Under federal and state law, health-care providers are, generally speaking, required to recognize and comply with a valid living will or power of attorney.

POWERS OF ATTORNEY

A power of attorney is a legal document in which the maker (the principal) gives another person (the agent, sometimes called the "attorney-in-fact") legal authority to act on her behalf under certain circumstances, which are spelled out in the document. Powers of attorney can be broad, or strictly limited to certain duties, such as making financial transactions or health-care decisions.

A power of attorney must be created and executed (in most places, this means signed and notarized) while the principal is legally competent. It usually remains in effect until it is revoked or the principal dies. Some powers granted by these documents carry special requirements in order to be effective. For example, in many places a power of attorney that allows the agent to sell real estate must be recorded in the office of the county clerk or recorder of deeds where the property is located. A power of attorney can't be used by an agent to take care of property transfers or avoid the tasks assigned to the probate process.

Some states provide forms for various types of powers of attorney, sometimes included within the state statutes. Standard forms are also available from other sources, such as nonprofit organizations (see Appendix) and through seminars on related topics. While completing a power of attorney is generally a simple task most people can do themselves, it is still wise to have your attorney look it over to make sure it meets all the requirements of your state's law. For example, some states require powers of attorney to be notarized.

If you move to another state, your power of attorney should still be honored as long as it met the requirements of the state in which it was executed. However, as with a will, it is best to make a new one that complies with the law of the state where you live. It is also important to review powers of attorney from time to time to be sure your needs and objectives remain the same. If you decide to make a new power of attorney, the old one should be revoked in writing, be notarized, and a copy should be sent to everyone who had a copy of the old one or who might otherwise be affected by it.

DURABLE POWERS OF ATTORNEY

A durable power of attorney is one that provides, by specific legal language, that the authority granted to the agent will take effect only if the principal becomes incapacitated, and will remain in effect for the duration of the principal's incapacity. The document should also contain a definition of what constitutes "incapacity." Many people prepare durable powers of attorney that give a spouse, partner, friend, adult child, or another the right to make health-care, financial, and/or other decisions should they become incapacitated and unable to do so themselves.

A durable power of attorney is a wise move. If you do not designate a person to handle these things for you if you cannot, the court is required to appoint someone. In choosing your own agent or agents, you can be sure that if the need ever arises, these key decisions will be made by someone you trust to carry out your wishes and make the same choices for you that you would have made for yourself.

Your agent may be any competent adult individual, or it may be a bank or other institution. Agents should be trustworthy and possess the required skills to carry out their duties. In some areas, there are organizations that serve as agents for a modest fee. Many people prepare two or more durable powers of attorney to appoint different agents to different tasks, for example, a family member to make health-care decisions and a bank to handle financial issues. Copies of each durable power of attorney should be provided to the agents and any alternate agents you may have designated, as well as to your physician, family members, attorney, and anyone else who might be affected if you become incapaciated and the need to use the power of attorney arises.

Sometimes the term *living will* is used interchangeably with a durable power of attorney for health care. However, these are generally different documents. A living will (discussed below) informs the doctor who will treat you should you be incapacitated of your wishes about life support.

Different states have different requirements for creating a durable power of attorney for health care and/or a living will. Most hospitals, and most estate planning attorneys, have forms that meet the requirements in your state. Some of the organizations listed in the Appendix also provide forms tailored to meet each state's requirements.

LIVING WILLS

In addition to specifying what type of care you wish to receive and who will make your decisions for you should you become incapacitated, a durable power of attorney combined with other directives—such as a living will—can also help protect your loved ones from a financial fiasco. Most health insurance policies have limits that set a maximum the policy will pay for health-care coverage. On the average, this is about $1 million. This sounds like a great deal of money, but it may be reached quickly if something happens that requires you to have long-term hospital care. Once the maximum is reached, it is your loved ones who must pick up the tab as the bills continue to grow.

Families are often torn apart when one member is injured or suffers an illness that renders them unconscious and incapacitated but does not kill them outright. In today's high-tech medical world, "life" may be sustained for years, even decades, by artificial means, although the person has no awareness of anything taking place around him, and all hope that he will regain his ability to enjoy or experience life is gone forever. In many such cases, the person may have clearly stated his wishes not to be kept alive by such means, and elicited a promise from his spouse that she would never allow this to happen. However, if other family members disagree about what should be done, such a promise is ineffective, unless the person's wishes were formalized in the appropriate written document. Families often battle in court for years to try to bring such a tragedy to a conclusion.

The U.S. Supreme Court has decided that competent people have the right to refuse life-prolonging medical treatment, as long as they understand the consequences of their decision. But if you want to be sure that your wishes are carried out in the event that you are unable to express them directly, it is important to be sure that your wishes are communicated in a manner that meets the requirements of your state's laws. In almost all states, a clearly written "living will" that plainly sets out when and what kind of life-prolonging treatment you do and do not want is legally effective, although the specific requirements of the states vary.

You, and only you, should have the right to decide what will happen to you if you reach the point where you are unable to make your own health-care decisions. Essentially, three options are available: First, you may want to specify that your life is to be prolonged no matter what, without regard to the likelihood of your recovery, physical or mental condition, or the cost of the treatment. Second, you may state that life-sustaining treatment is to be continued unless you are in a coma or a persistent vegetative state, as documented by two doctors—one of whom is your regular physician—who have examined you and determined in their best judgment that there is little chance you will recover. Third, you may specify that you do not want your life to be unnaturally prolonged, unless there is a reasonable degree of hope that your physical and mental health will be restored.

Your living will should also name a person who will act as your agent (or more than one person to act as co-agents, as many recommend) to ensure that your wishes are carried out. It is important to name people who care about you but are strong enough to make the wrenching decision to see that your preferences are followed. Once you have completed this document, be sure that your doctor and the named agents have copies.

Although creating a durable power of attorney or living will requires facing difficult and morbid possibilities, it should not be put off. As financial planner and author Suze Orman states, "The moment you need to do this document, it is too late to create it."

FUNERAL, BURIAL, AND ORGAN-DONATION PLANS

More and more people today are planning their own funerals. Making a conscious decision about this squeamish subject while you are able to state your preferences can not only give you peace of mind but can also save your loved ones a great deal of grief and inconvenience.

Preplanning can also save your estate and your family a substantial sum of money. The average cost of a conventional funeral in the United States is about $7,000. Making arrangements in advance can help your loved ones avoid this tremendous expense through pre-payment, and by excluding any components of the conventional funeral that you do not wish to be included. It also allows you to plan for the type of service that has dignity and meaning for you, and spare your family the necessity of having to make decisions at a time when they are confused and upset.

Death is an uneasy subject in our culture, but if you are willing to grit your teeth and do a small amount of work as a part of your estate planning, you can be assured that your wishes are carried out and your family won't be faced with awkward dilemmas, for example, learning that your desire to have your ashes scattered in a particular place is not legal, or a situation in which one family member insists on an elaborate funeral, while another prefers a simple service.

Even if you want a traditional funeral, preplanning and comparing options offered by various funeral homes can save you and your family a great deal of money. Various organizations offer information and services to assist with preplanning (see Appendix). It is always a good idea to specify the type of service or ceremony you do or do not wish to have after your death, even if your feelings are not particularly strong on this matter. If you are affiliated with a particular church or other religious institution, you may state that you want to follow the traditional ritual, perhaps listing songs or prayers, and naming a priest, pastor, or rabbi whom you would like to conduct the service. If you want a memorial that is more individualized or unusual, write down your specific request for it.

You may also wish to leave instructions about what is not to be done with your body. For instance, the traditional open-casket visitation and drawn-out funeral can be a horrible ordeal, so I have left instructions requesting no viewing, and prompt cremation, followed by a simple service in line with my own spiritual beliefs. Others, however, feel that a traditional funeral service is beneficial and important, and have chosen to leave detailed instructions, even specifying how their body is to be clothed for the service. This is an entirely personal choice each individual should be allowed to make. However, unless you state your intentions in writing, the burden will be on your loved ones to guess what you would have wanted. Also, in some places, it can be difficult to arrange a cremation if any family member objects, unless the decedent's instructions are clearly stated in writing.

Many people also choose to name a particular charity to which donations should be made, sometimes in lieu of flowers at the funeral.

It is also becoming increasingly common for people to write their own death notices and/or obituaries as a part of their instructions. This is another step that can lighten the burden on loved ones who will need to provide this information to the appropriate local newspaper. It can be difficult to face this chore immediately after a person's death, as well as to remember all the required details, such as place of birth and names of parents and siblings. Books, such as *Last Wishes* by Lucinda Pagge Knox, or pamphlets from various organizations (see Appendix) can help you compile the necessary information and take other important steps in funeral preplanning.

Many people overlook the importance of this facet of estate planning. Given the astronomical costs and strong emotions involved, funeral planning is an essential component. Your instructions may be contained in your will, or they may be in the form of written burial instructions that, under the law of most states, are binding as long as they don't violate state laws on the disposition of bodies (such as requesting burial in a place other than a cemetery). Some advise preparing this instrument as a separate document, even if the instructions are repeated in the will, because bodies must be dealt with quickly, and it can take awhile to find and process a will. Make sure that the person who will be responsible for carrying out your wishes after your death has a copy of your instructions, or at least knows where to find them.

Donating Organs and Tissue

If you wish to donate organs and tissue, it is important to execute the proper documents *before* your death. All states have now adopted the Uniform Anatomical Gift Act, which provides that any mentally competent adult can fill out a simple form stipulating organ donations after death. Some states have incorporated this process into driver's licensing and renewal. Your estate planning attorney, physician, or certain national organizations listed in the Appendix—such as the Living Bank—can provide the correct documents. Again, it is important that your family and close friends, as well as your doctor, are aware of your wishes, because successful removal of donated body parts must be done very quickly after death.

If you want to donate your entire body to medical research, this must also be arranged in advance, with alternatives in case the donation is refused (as sometimes happens for various reasons).

ELDER LAW ISSUES RELATED TO ESTATE PLANNING

Such topics as long-term-care insurance, Medicare/Medicaid laws, pension benefits, and retirement plans actually fall within a field of legal specialization called "elder law" rather than under the headings of probate law or estate planning. Yet, not surprisingly, there is a great deal of overlap in these two specialties, both for the practical reason that as people grow older they naturally become more concerned about estate planning; and because planning your estate often requires considering the impact of beneficiary-designating insurance and retirement plans upon a person's overall estate plan.

A word of caution: Individual needs and circumstances vary, and options and laws in this area are in a state of flux. Seek the advice of a qualified elder law attorney and/or senior citizens advocate in assessing your own needs—and be aware that while some attorneys have specialized knowledge in both estate planning and elder law, they are separate fields with limited overlap. Be sure you seek qualified assistance in both areas.

Long-Term–Care Insurance, Medicare, and Medicaid

Long-term-care (LTC) insurance is simply nursing home insurance. Most people don't like to contemplate the possibility that they will need this type of care, but realistically, millions of people do require some form of assisted living during the later years of their lives, and nursing home care can be astronomically expensive. Some financial advisers, such as author Suze Orman, believe that long-term-care insurance is one of the most important types people can buy, both for their own peace of mind and to protect the assets of their estate. Orman reports that she advises all her clients older than fifty to consider purchasing LTC insurance.

LTC insurance is not available to everyone. For example, those with significant health problems cannot obtain it. But for those who can purchase such coverage, it can help provide them a higher quality of nursing home care should they need it, as well as protecting their spouse from losing all of his assets to pay for their care. This is a devastating result faced by many couples who have worked hard to plan for retirement. Good nursing home care may run several thousands of dollars per month, a sum that can quickly eat up all of a family's savings, retirement income, and other assets.

Orman also emphasizes that LTC insurance is separate and distinct from health insurance. No health insurance policy in existence covers long-term care. A separate LTC insurance policy must be added. Sometimes group insurance plans, offered through an employer or otherwise, offer LTC insurance. If you are eligible for such a plan, be sure to ask about LTC.

As Orman and other experts point out, many people expect that Medicare or Medicaid will pick up the tab for nursing home care. However, Medicare pays only the first twenty days of an LTC stay at Medicare-approved skilled-nursing facilities. Only 1 percent of all the people in nursing homes today are in skilled-nursing homes, while the other 99 percent are in homes that provide custodial care, not the twenty-four-hour-a-day R.N. services required by Medicare, Orman explains. Medicare pays for less than 2 percent of all the people in nursing homes today.

Medicaid, the federally administered program run by the individual states, only covers those who are defined—under official terms—as financially destitute. For the truly destitute, this may be the only option, but for those who attempt to divest their assets in order to become eligible for Medicaid, I offer several words of caution: First, both the law and administration system surrounding Medicaid change rapidly, and are currently in a state of flux. Some believe that a new version of the former "granny goes to jail law," discussed earlier, could be enacted. Many predict that by the time the baby boomers reach the age at which they'll need nursing care, Medicaid will no longer exist. Also, Medicaid-approved nursing facilities are not always the best. In fact, they are frequently overburdened and underfunded.

The bottom line is: We must all consider the fact that we may someday be unable to care for ourselves as we can today. And none of us can count on other family members, or the government, to take care of us. LTC insurance makes sense for nearly everyone. The law is changing to support LTC insurance, with corporations that pay for LTC coverage for their employees now being allowed to deduct the cost of the premiums as a company business expense. Employer-paid LTC is not taxable to the employee, and individuals can consider it a medical expense. For self-employed people, LTC insurance may also be deducted as a business expense. Again, the law is changing rapidly, so be sure to get sound advice about your options for deducting these premiums. You can call the Health Insurance Counseling and Advocacy Program, at 1-800-434-0222, for a referral to an office in your area.

Types of policies and what they offer vary, so be sure that you discuss your LTC options with a qualified insurance professional. As with any form of insurance, be sure that you can afford it today, as well as after you retire. Also, bear in mind that assistance to the elderly varies from state to state, as do LTC policies in terms of cost, coverage, eligibility requirements, and the stability of the company that sells them. A particularly important clause for many people is the home-health care clause, which allows you to receive your benefits for short-term care at home.

Don't shy away from LTC insurance because of these complexities. It is well worth the time and energy to acquire the right plan, so that you can avoid the devastation of being wiped out financially, or see your spouse suffer such a fate when you are in your seventies or eighties.

■ Chapter 5

Living Trusts

Four types of property can pass to your beneficiaries without going through the court-supervised probate system: First, life insurance and certain other beneficiary accounts, such as annuities and IRAs that are directly payable to the named beneficiary; second, property jointly owned with a right of survivorship, such as pay-on-death bank accounts and real estate held in joint tenancy; third, gifts made during your lifetime to people or organizations; and finally, property held in any type of trust other than a testamentary trust (a trust within a will, discussed in chapter 4).

Various types of trusts used in estate planning accomplish different purposes. Trusts can be a good way to manage your assets during your lifetime and efficiently transfer them to your beneficiaries after your death. They can preserve privacy, while allowing continued control of your assets. Trusts can also result in tax savings, both before and after death. One of the most popular and common forms of trusts used in estate planning is the revocable "inter vivos" or "living" trust. Living trusts are discussed in this chapter. (The other types of non-probate transfer are covered in chapter 6.)

A living trust is a written agreement between the individual creating the trust (called the "trustor," "grantor," or "settlor"), and a person or an institution that will manage the assets held in trust (called the "trustee"). The trust itself functions as a separate legal entity that owns the assets transferred to it. Like a will, the trust specifies where each piece of property will go after you die. Then the trust passes your property directly to your beneficiaries without the involvement of the probate court.

Technically, living trusts are known under the law as "revocable inter vivos" trusts. Revocable means that the person who establishes the trust can revoke or change any part or all of it. Inter vivos is a Latin term that means "during life." This means that the trust is set up while the person is living. Thus, a living trust may be amended or revoked at anytime during the maker's lifetime, as long as he is legally competent to do so.

CREATING A LIVING TRUST

Two steps are required to create a living trust. First, the trust is established as a legal entity, then assets are transferred into it (sometimes called funding the trust). The required steps may often be accomplished simultaneously.

Transfer of assets into the trust is accomplished in different ways for different types of property. With real estate, a new deed that transfers ownership of the property to the trust is prepared. For automobiles and other vehicles, a trip to the local motor vehicle office to transfer title is required. Much of this work can be done by the client, but it is probably best to have an attorney prepare deeds for real property, to make sure that they are drafted and recorded correctly. Attorneys often take care of deeds for clients, as well as prepare an assignment of tangible personal property, to transfer things like art, jewelry, and antiques into trust ownership. This is a simple one-page document that lists the property. For stocks and similar types of property, the client should talk to his broker or the person who manages the stock. For your own stock, you may need to speak with the transfer agent. As for bank accounts, most banks have their own forms. If you take a copy of the trust agreement to your bank, a bank officer can help you prepare the required documents. Financial advisers can be a great help, as well. Today, living trusts are common, so most professionals who work in these fields are familiar with how they work.

While it requires some paperwork to place assets into a living trust, it is usually easy to transfer assets in or out of the trust once it is set up. However, mistakes occur. Hiring a lawyer to handle these transfers means another fee, but it is often worth the price to be certain that the transfer is done correctly if you have any qualms about making these changes yourself. At any rate, it is important to achieve these transfers quickly and correctly, according to the requirements of each state's laws (such as real-estate recording statutes) and the rules of each financial institution.

As Suze Orman explains in her best-selling book, *The 9 Steps to Financial Freedom,* a living trust is like a suitcase. You put the title to your house, stocks, and other property in it, along with the designation of who will own it after you are gone. While you are alive, you carry the suitcase with you and are free to put new things in or take things out. When you die, the suitcase is handed directly to your beneficiaries.

Generally speaking, everything you own except your retirement accounts may be transferred into your living trust. The law requires that retirement accounts must be held in an individual's name, however, the beneficiary of a retirement account may be the trust, so that assets in the account are funneled through the trust at the appropriate time. I would caution married couples that while a spouse has the legal right to take over the other spouse's retirement account if one dies, and continue to have all the rights and privileges they had under the account, this right is lost if the account is left to anyone else as the beneficiary—including parents, children, or a trust. In nearly all cases, any such beneficiary other than one's spouse is required to take the money out and pay taxes on it within a five-year period. This is true even if a husband or wife is the only beneficiary under the trust. If the retirement funds go through the trust, the special right to take over the account is wiped out. Many advise structuring a retirement account so that a spouse is named as the primary beneficiary, with the trust named as the secondary beneficiary to receive the money in the account if the primary beneficiary dies before you do.

TRUSTORS AND TRUSTEES

Usually, the trustor (the person who sets up the trust and owns the property in it) is the same person as the trustee. However, you may name other trustees ("cotrustees"), such as your spouse, who share authority to manage and use the assets in the trust. All trustees must generally agree to financial or investment changes. Adult children are often named as cotrustees, so that they may take over management of the assets if their parents become disabled or do not wish to have this responsibility as they get older.

A cotrustee should be distinguished from a successor trustee. A successor trustee is a person who is named to step in and make decisions about the trust assets *only* if the trustee or cotrustees cannot or choose not to make these decisions. Again, adult children are often named as successor trustees, allowing them to take over management of the assets when their parent no longer wants the burden of making these decisions.

Living trusts usually name a specific successor trustee to handle the business of wrapping up the trustor's estate and distributing assets to the beneficiaries when the trustor dies. This successor trustee performs essentially the same duties as a personal representative for someone who has a will. For those with both a will and a living trust, the same person or institution may act as both PR and successor trustee.

One who serves as any type of trustee occupies a special legal position, known as a "fiduciary." This person has a heightened duty of trust and confidence, and is subject to strict responsibilities and higher standards of performance than a person or institution who does not occupy this role. The trustee must hold the trust property solely for the benefit of the trust's beneficiaries, and may not use the property for his own personal use, benefit, or self-interest, unless the settlor gives express permission to do so in writing.

BENEFICIARIES

Trust beneficiaries fall into two categories: current beneficiaries, usually the person who created the trust and owns the property placed in it; and remainder beneficiaries, those who inherit the assets in the trust after the current beneficiary dies. Beneficiaries of the trust may include yourself (it is not uncommon for the same person to be trustor, trustee, and beneficiary), your family, or anyone else you designate.

HOW DOES A LIVING TRUST WORK?

For many people who create a living trust simply as an estate planning tool, this transfer of ownership is merely a "legal fiction" that serves to restructure the way property is owned, so that they may avoid probate, and in some cases, enjoy other benefits as described below.

An example can help make this more clear. A married couple, Jonas and Rasheeda Butler, creates a living trust and transfers their home, two vehicles, and personal goods to the trust. Title to this property is signed over to the trust for the Butlers' own use and benefit while they are alive, and for their named beneficiaries after they die. The Butlers still use, manage, and control this property exactly as they did before they set up the trust.

A revocable living trust can also be amended at any time, so it is relatively simple to change your mind about who will get what assets when you are gone or to make other adjustments. For example, if the Butlers have children, they can amend their trust to name the kids as beneficiaries. Perhaps they buy another home but keep their original home as rental property.

This house is now an income-producing asset of the trust, and the trustees are responsible for distributing the income to the beneficiaries. If the Butlers are their own trustees and beneficiaries, they simply collect the rent money and "distribute" it to themselves. Or, they may prefer to appoint a bank, for example, or a property-management company, as cotrustee to collect the rent and forward it to them.

Many people worry that in setting up a trust they are giving up their own power to manage their assets, and placing that power in someone else's hands. In the case of a revocable living trust, this is not true. Most people continue to manage their assets in the same way they did before setting up the trust, as trustee. You may also continue to hold property you and your spouse own as a joint tenant or as community property. Bear in mind that some states, such as New York, have certain restrictions that may prevent the same person from acting as trustee and beneficiary, or other laws that will affect the way the trust must be set up. Check with an attorney in your home state, as well as someone who knows the law in the state where the property is located, before completing any trust.

ADVANTAGES OF A LIVING TRUST

A living trust may have several advantages over a will. The most important are:

Avoiding the Delay and Expense of Probate

First and foremost, when all your property is transferred through a living trust, there is no probate procedure, and the courts are not involved in distributing your estate. Depending on where you die, this can save your estate a great deal of time and money by freeing it from the obligation of going through the probate process and paying the attendant legal fees.

To avoid probate, with a few exceptions, the title to all of a settlor's assets must be transferred into the trust. Certain assets with a value of a set amount under state law (for example, $60,000 in California) do not need to be transferred into the trust in order to avoid probate. Also, assets held in joint tenancy, or those that pass by beneficiary designation, such as life insurance, do not have to be transferred into the trust to avoid probate.

When establishing a living trust, many attorneys routinely prepare a "pourover will," which, as we've explained, is a simple document that serves as a safety valve in case an individual who intended to transfer all her assets into a living trust forgets anything, or acquires property after she has set up the trust and does not transfer it before her death. The cost of a pourover will is minimal, the document simple, and there is no need to probate the will if the person transferred everything into the living trust, as intended. But if it does turn out that she owned other property, the pourover will is a simple way to make sure that it goes where she wants it to go and doesn't pass by intestate succession.

Privacy

When a will is filed for probate with the court, it becomes a public document that anyone can read in the court file. A trust, in contrast, is a private document. What you own and how you choose to distribute your estate remain your own business. This may be especially important for those with substantial wealth or those who fear a disgruntled relative might try to make trouble if she became aware of the details of your estate plan. This is also important for people with sensitive privacy issues, such as gays or lesbians who do not want the details of their personal lives made public.

In most cases, the privacy factor is not a major issue. But for someone with a degree of celebrity or with complex family issues, it can be important. Anyone who anticipates that certain family members may snoop around to see if they got their fair share, or bickers over how the estate was distributed may want to consider this factor. However, some transfers, such as real estate, are always a matter of public record.

Trusts Are Less Frequently Contested

"The possibility that a living trust will be contested seems to be less likely than with a will," attorney Ruth Cohen observes. "Since a trust is a document that is drafted for use during your lifetime, as well as for distributing your estate after death, it is less likely that someone will argue that you were pressured in some way, as is often the basis for will contests."

Of course, trusts can be challenged, and sometimes lawsuits are filed. But estate contests over trusts apparently do not occur as often, and are harder to win simply because of the way a trust is legally structured.

Organizing and Consolidating Assets

For individuals with scattered property, a living trust may have definite advantages over a will, even in a state where probate is relatively simple. When someone owns land in more than one state, each parcel must be subject to an ancillary probate proceeding in the state where it is located. In that case, probate costs add up, so it can be a big advantage to place this land in trust. For example, those who own oil and gas interests—which are considered real estate—often have small parcels of real property that are spread out over several states. This can add a lot of time, effort, and expense if each must be transferred through an ancillary probate proceeding. It can be helpful to put these interests into living trusts. Cases have occurred in which the cost of probating a number of small oil and gas properties exceeded their value.

For some people, the peace of mind of knowing that their assets are organized in one place and will not have to pass through probate is worth a small amount of extra work and cost to see that everything is in order. For most people with few assets, the only great benefit of a living trust is avoiding probate. But for some people, having their assets organized, a successor trustee named, and everything orderly is important. For others, a trust makes them feel boxed in. Even though they retain control over their assets, they feel a slight loss of freedom. It is really up to the individual and his own sensibilities.

Appointing Alternate Trustees to Manage Assets

A living trust also enables the maker to have her assets managed during her lifetime, if such management becomes necessary. For example, if you become incompetent, a living trust, plus other estate-planning documents designating someone to manage your affairs, may enable you to avoid a conservatorship proceeding in court, in which the court must act to appoint someone to take care of you and your property.

For an older person who may wish to turn over management of his assets to an adult child or other person in the foreseeable future, it can be efficient to create a trust in which that person is named cotrustee. With a living trust, it is a simple process to appoint someone else, such as an adult child, to manage your assets as trustee if you wish to appoint someone else to oversee these tasks as you get older. This may be especially important for a person who has, for example, a history of Alzheimer's disease in the family. A properly worded living trust can make the succession of asset management easy, because there is no need to appoint a conservator or guardian for a person who becomes disabled. This can save money and time, and the individual who creates the living trust retains control over his property as his own trustee until the time comes when he is no longer able to do so.

Generally, passing authority to a cotrustee is a simple matter of changing the name of the trustee, then in writing, informing all the institutions that hold your money of the new trustee's name. This can also give a person an opportunity to see how a cotrustee performs in the role, so if it does not work out, she can name another cotrustee, or simply have an opportunity to make sure that the person performs the job well before she turns over management of her property.

For a living trust to fill this function, you must have placed your assets in the trust and named your cotrustees before you become incapacitated, or set up another device for doing so. However, a durable power of attorney can be used in some cases to achieve the same result for a lower cost. The key is to work with an experienced estate-planning attorney and evaluate all your options and alternatives before adopting any estate planning strategy.

Protecting the Estate from Creditors

When a will is filed for probate, creditors who have a claim against the decedent's estate have only a short time, specified by the state's probate statute, in which to file any claims. These limits are known as "non-claim statutes." Once this period has passed, most creditors are forever barred from making any further claim, and the assets can pass to the beneficiaries free and clear.

Depending upon the state, a living trust may offer an estate more protection against creditors by making the assets almost unreachable, at least to unsecured creditors (those whose interest is not secured by an interest in property, such as a mortgage on a home or a lien on a vehicle). In some states, creditors simply cannot touch assets in a living trust. In others, probate assets must be exhausted before creditors can levy claims against assets held in trust. In some jurisdictions, however, creditors of the trust maker can claim against assets in a living trust in essentially the same manner they can claim against probate property. And if a creditor can prove that a debtor used a living trust for abusive purposes—that is, solely to try to avoid his legitimate debts—there are methods that allow creditors to have the trust set aside, either while the maker is living or after his death.

Most states have statutes of limitations on the amount of time a creditor has to assert a claim against trust property. In most cases, these statutes allow creditors more time than the non-claim statutes of limitation that apply to wills. However, it is best to avoid this issue altogether by ensuring that you have adequate life insurance or other assets to satisfy all the legitimate claims that your creditors are likely to levy against your estate.

LIVING TRUSTS ARE NOT FOR EVERYONE

Each individual has different property issues, personal needs, and concerns that may determine whether a living trust is the right choice. The advantages and disadvantages of different estate plan options should be discussed thoroughly with a qualified estate planning attorney. The living trust is, in itself, a neutral document. Whether a person should have a will, a living trust, or both depends on her individual situation.

Probate costs and complexities vary greatly from state to state, which may affect the choice of a living trust over a will. Some people believe that they will save attorney's fees by choosing a living trust over a will. In a state with slow and costly probate procedures, this may be true when a person dies and his estate must be distributed. However, it usually costs about the same to have a will or trust drafted, although preparation of a living trust may be slightly more expensive, because of the need to transfer title to property into the trust. Again, this depends on the individual's estate.

"The main disadvantage of creating a living trust is cost," attorney Cohen observes. "For clients with fairly simple estates, for whom probate costs are not likely to be high, and where privacy is not a major issue, the added expense may outweigh the benefits."

LIVING TRUSTS DO NOT AVOID OR LOWER ESTATE TAXES

Estate taxes are discussed in more detail in the next chapter, but it is important to clarify a common misunderstanding regarding estate taxes and living trusts. Many people mistakenly believe that by placing their assets into a living trust, they are automatically subject to lower estate taxes than if they had transferred the same assets through a will. This is not true.

Estate planning attorneys emphasize that a living trust has no effect on whether property will be subject to estate taxes. Other types of trusts, discussed in the next chapter, may be effectively used to reduce estate taxes, and estate tax savings provisions can be incorporated into living trusts. These provisions can also be included in a will.

The primary advantage of a living trust as opposed to a will is to avoid or reduce probate costs. It is a tax-neutral document, with no estate tax advantage.

Although there is no probate of property that passes through a living trust, the successor trustee is still required to file income and estate tax returns as a part of completing the legal administrative and asset-transfer chores.

Chapter 6

Life Insurance, Jointly Owned Property, and Other Non-Probate Transfers

Different types of estate-planning tools serve different purposes. A complete estate plan often comprises a number of components, all of which work together to achieve the various goals of a good plan.

LIFE INSURANCE

"Normally, it is important to have life insurance, because nothing else pays immediately when a person dies," explains Caroline Hallett, owner of Hallett Insurance Agency and representative of the Principal Financial Group. "Life insurance provides the money that is needed immediately for burial expenses and other costs. For those whose estates are valued in excess of $650,000, it is also important to have life insurance to cover estate tax obligations."

However, Hallett does not believe that everyone needs life insurance. "For some people, a pension plan or other arrangement provides enough," she explains. "But for most, life insurance is an essential component of estate planning, and may provide other benefits as well, such as a payback for retirement."

As Hallett notes, those who are single and have no dependents really have little or no need for any type of life insurance. Yet she urges clients to consider life insurance while they are still young. "People younger than thirty seldom give life insurance much thought, but the sooner you buy, the sooner you tie yourself in to being able to get a substantial amount of life insurance for a reasonable price. For example, I may advise a recently married twenty-five-year-old client who plans to have a family in the next few years to go ahead and purchase a $250,000 term policy. That way, the policy is tied in, so her family's needs are protected even if, for example, she develops health problems later."

If you currently contribute to someone's support, it is essential to understand the different types of life insurance and how to figure out how much and which type you need. "In addition to providing immediate cash to pay burial and related expenses when a person dies, life insurance serves two main purposes," Hallett explains. "The life insurance benefits should be sufficient to pay off outstanding debt and to replace income. The lost income is the most important consideration for a person with a family. However, this is also an important factor for people who are older and living on retirement income. Often, lost retirement is not figured in when people try to determine how much life insurance they need. A standard rule is that life insurance should cover at least 70 percent of the income a person would earn between the time of death and the time his youngest child reaches the age of majority. However, a good planner has more sophisticated methods of calculating what a person really needs, depending on each individual's circumstances."

An individual's family situation has a major impact on the type of life insurance plan that is best, Hallett states. "In addition to paying the 'final expenses,' including funeral costs, the purpose of death benefits is to provide a cushion for your family. We have discussed the primary purposes of replacing income and paying off debt, but families with children also need to consider such costs as future education."

The first step in calculating how much life insurance your family needs to carry on without financial hardship if something happened to you is to understand your family's current expenses. Books such as Suze Orman's *The 9 Steps to Financial Freedom* or Judy Lawrence's *The Budget Kit* provide easy-to-use charts to help you calculate the monthly obligations you face today. The advantage of using such a tool is that we often forget costs that are not billed every month, such as quarterly insurance premiums or we underestimate the total, annual charges that accumulate for such things as children's music lessons, sports activities, etc.

In calculating your expenses to determine your life insurance requirements, it is also a good idea to ponder how your family's needs might change if you were no longer there. For example, if you are a mother who works part-time outside your home and spends your remaining hours devoted to child care, while your husband works full-time, he would not only lose the benefit of your income, but he would also have to pay more for child care. If you are your home's primary caretaker, he may also need to spend more for housekeeping services or eating out, for example. It is not pleasant to consider, but realistically, those who face the unexpected death of a spouse may also need to pay for mental health counseling, more frequent trips to visit family members, and long-distance telephone costs to find the necessary comfort from loved ones to help them through their grief. Of course, such expenses can't be calculated to the penny, but it is a good idea to have a general overview of how your death would impact your family's current and future financial situation.

Some experts advise buying approximately $100,000 in life insurance for every $500 you must bring in each month to cover your share of the household expenses. For example, if you are the sole breadwinner for a household that requires $4,000 a month to cover all its costs, according to this formula, you would need $800,000 in life insurance. This is based on the idea that your beneficiary should be able to invest the insurance money at a rate of about 6 percent per year and earn enough money to cover household expenses without having to dip into the principal—so that your income would be replaced forever.

Realistically, however, many people cannot afford to buy this much insurance. Your needs also depend upon your own situation. For example, if you are self-employed and are still using most of your income to pay off start-up debts on your business while contributing relatively little to the overall household budget, assuming your insurance would be sufficient to pay off all your outstanding business debts and replace the portion you do contribute to the household, you should use a different formula. If your children are in their last years of college and, hopefully, are about to become self-supporting, this will also affect your calculations. Or, for example, if you spend a large portion of your own income on an expensive hobby or interest your family does not share and would not continue if you were gone, this income would not need to be replaced.

Bear in mind, also, that individuals vary greatly in their financial comfort zone. Some of us feel flush with wealth if there is a fifty dollar surplus in the checking account after we have paid our monthly bills. For others, the sight of their savings account dipping below the sum required to cover all of their needs for the next two years fills them with immediate panic. In contemplating how much life insurance to buy, the final decision should be based upon a balance struck between how much it would take to make your family feel secure and how much you can realistically afford to pay at the current time.

Many people make the mistake of relying on employer-sponsored life insurance alone. Hallett cautions clients that the life insurance offered through an employer should always be considered temporary and viewed as nothing more than a supplement to the total insurance portfolio. "If you decide to leave your job or change careers, this insurance will no longer be available," she explains. "And this can be a source of major problems. For example, I know of one person who had cancer two years ago and now wants to change jobs. Even though she is cured, it will be hard for her to get life insurance now, so she has chosen to stay in a job where she isn't happy, so that she can keep her insurance."

A change in jobs can also mean the loss of accumulated retirement income. A type of life insurance now generally referred to as "permanent" can provide an insurance payout upon death, as well as a supplemental source of income after the policyholder reaches retirement age.

Term Versus Permanent Life Insurance

Life insurance comes in two basic categories. "Term" life insurance is the type most of us are more familiar with. When you buy a term policy, you pay yearly premiums, usually at a fixed rate, for a set number of years. If you die during this term, your family or other designated beneficiaries receive a specific amount of money. If you live until the term of the policy expires, you receive nothing. "Permanent" life insurance refers to any of several types of life insurance (including "whole life," "variable," or "universal life") which, in addition to paying a death benefit, provides a return on the money paid in as premiums, after a certain period of time has elapsed. The premiums are higher than those paid on a term policy, because the policy combines insurance with an investment program that can provide retirement income.

Term insurance is just that—insurance that is available for a set term, the life of the policy, and which then expires. This is why the premiums for term insurance are usually fairly inexpensive. The insurance company gambles that you will not die during the term of your policy. Term insurance is available in different length terms, many of which are automatically renewable. For many renewable policies, the premiums increase as the policy expires and is then renewed. Many policies run for five, ten, or up to twenty years, during which time the premium is fixed. In today's highly competitive insurance market, companies are offering new deals all the time, so be sure to study your options.

While Hallett believes that for most it is wise to allot a portion of life insurance premiums for investment toward retirement income, she acknowledges that in the short run it is also important to keep premiums reasonable. "Term insurance and permanent insurance can be blended to make it more affordable," she explains. "It is important that we be able to offer this type of product, but the greatest concern is still to have an adequate face amount, so that the death benefit paid if a person dies unexpectedly is sufficient to meet the main objectives of paying debt and replacing income."

Hallett advises many clients to begin with term insurance alone. "This is the simplest type of life insurance, the kind most people are familiar with," she explains. "It is like renting: Money is put into the policy, and in return, a death benefit is paid out when you die. Permanent life insurance can be compared to buying a home with a mortgage. Cash is accumulated, and there is always some return. But it may be a low- to high percentage, depending upon the risk involved."

Universal life insurance is a species of permanent insurance in which the rate of return is variable. A permanent policy can be a very good thing, but make sure you understand all the factors involved, and remember that the death benefit is the most important component of any life insurance policy. "Most people don't need to have all their life insurance in a permanent policy, and each individual needs to consider his own situation and requirements." Those interested in some form of permanent life insurance should talk to a qualified insurance professional about the options available, Hallet advises. "There are many different kinds of permanent life insurance today."

A person who does not expect to have much retirement income from another source should consider a permanent policy to supplement this income. "Life insurance is almost always a part of a good estate plan, but the kind you will need depends on your future aspirations," says Hallett. "The vehicle that funds your particular insurance plan will also depend upon your risk tolerance. Annuities have a lower risk factor than most mutual funds and other stock accounts. With some types of life insurance, you can use your own investments chosen through mutual funds, but for most people, no more than 50 percent of their life insurance should be funded by a vehicle with substantial risk attached. Don't try to fund a retirement plan for twenty years from now, until you have taken care of what might happen tomorrow."

Some financial experts advise that whole life or universal policies are a relatively poor way to save money or structure a retirement plan, because in addition to the money you are paying in for savings, you are also paying the agent a huge commission.

For others, however, especially those who have a difficult time saving money, some form of permanent life insurance may be the right choice. If you are considering this route, shop around to compare premiums; to make sure the premiums are reasonable and affordable, to work with a reputable agent and company; and, most importantly, that you understand exactly what you are buying and what you are risking. Your agent will show you a chart or graphic that illustrates what your premium will buy. Remember, the money you pay in will be invested, and the risk attached to different types of investment varies tremendously. Each chart or illustration has a projected-earnings column, as well as a guaranteed-earnings column. Projected earnings are a "best-case" scenario, while guaranteed earnings show the lowest death benefit and interest rate the company can pay you. Focus your attention on this column. You should be comfortable with this, the "worst-case" scenario, and understand it thoroughly. A responsible agent will always take the time to explain these minimums thoroughly, whether you ask or not.

Reassess Your Insurance Needs from Time to Time

Life insurance needs change as you get older. As mentioned, most people need less life insurance once their children are self-supporting adults. If you have a sound retirement plan, you probably will not need life insurance at all past age sixty-five. However, never cancel a policy until you are certain that your spouse or other dependents no longer need it, and until you are certain that you will not need the policy for any reason in the future, since life insurance is more costly and difficult to obtain as you get older, or if you develop health problems.

Shop Around for Life Insurance

Today more than ever, insurance is a competitive business. Rates often vary astronomically for the same insurance coverage, whether life or another type. (See the Appendix for a list of services that provides quotes to help you find the best priced policy for the insurance you need.) Be sure you have calculated how much insurance and the type you need before you call these services, so that you have the information they require. Some advise checking with several of the services, since their quotes often vary.

Life Insurance Benefits and Your Estate

It is important to understand how life insurance death benefits may impact your estate. While insurance benefits are not taxable as a beneficiary's income, this money is considered a part of your estate and therefore subject to federal estate taxes if it is large enough to trigger them (as of 1999, this means a total estate value of $650,000 or more). Many people of middle-class means may not dream that their estate exceeds this limit, but when the value of a home, vehicles, a few family heirlooms, and a hefty life insurance benefit is combined, you may be worth more than you know. In calculating the value of your estate, consider the combined present value of all your assets (remember, real estate tends to appreciate sharply in some areas), plus all your life insurance policies.

Caroline Hallett also emphasizes the importance of ensuring that an adequate plan is in place to deal with any estate taxes that may be levied. "Many of my older clients should be concerned about estate taxes," she says. "The first step is to figure out what their estate taxes will total, then work with an attorney to determine, if possible, how to minimize them. Then we can be sure that what is left is funded with life insurance, so that the family won't have to have a fire sale to pay taxes when the person dies. Again, this is the same theme, of paying off debts and protecting income."

PENSIONS, RETIREMENT ACCOUNTS, AND OTHER BENEFICIAL PLANS

In addition to life insurance, pensions, annuities, and similar accounts usually provide a death benefit that is not subject to probate. However, such benefits may affect the taxable value of your estate, are often subject to marital property laws (such as community property ownership), and may require special handling to accomplish your goals. So it is important to understand and consider the effect of such accounts on your total estate planning picture.

The law that governs retirement and similar accounts is complex and changes frequently. It is generally considered a component of elder law rather than estate planning, yet the two are closely intertwined. As you put together or revise your estate plan, you may need to consult with your plan administrator. This person should be able to answer your questions about your specific account, but you may also need to contact a public or private senior-services agency, and/or an elder law attorney (some lawyers are well versed in both fields, while others specialize in one or the other) for specific information on how your retirement accounts might impact on your overall estate plan.

A Word of Caution About Beneficiary Designations

Many people do not realize that a will, trust, or other estate planning document that names certain individuals to receive the proceeds of the estate does not override any beneficiary designation you may have made on your employee benefits, 401(k) retirement accounts, or life insurance policies. If you wish the proceeds of any such benefits to go to someone other than the person designated in the account document, you must change the document itself. It is a good idea to review the beneficiary designations on such accounts anytime you create or update an estate plan, to ensure that all of the designations match. If you have a variety of packages and plans, be careful to confirm that each beneficiary designation is correct. You should also understand how each plan impacts your overall estate situation.

Also, as discussed in the last chapter, your spouse usually has the legal right to take over your retirement account if you die, and continue to have all of the rights and privileges you had under the account—especially tax deferral. But if someone other than your spouse, as an individual, is named as the beneficiary of the account when you die, this right is lost. In nearly all cases, this means that if you name a living trust as beneficiary of the retirement account, with your spouse as beneficiary of the trust, then she will lose the special rights enjoyed only by a beneficiary spouse. This is true even if your husband or wife is the only beneficiary under the trust. Many professionals advise structuring a retirement account so that your spouse is named as the primary beneficiary, with the trust named as the secondary beneficiary to receive the money in the account if the primary beneficiary dies before you do.

JOINTLY OWNED PROPERTY

For many people, the most inexpensive and efficient way to transfer real estate (and in some instances, other types of property) is through setting up joint ownership with your spouse, partner, parent, or child. This may be done when property is acquired, or at a later time.

The manner in which you own and hold title to your assets can have a significant effect upon your estate planning goals. As you create or reassess your estate plan, examine the manner in which you currently hold title to your property. A change in the structure of your ownership can, in some situations, avoid probate or lower your income and other taxes. For example, if a couple lives in a home that one person owned before the marriage, the home must pass through probate if that person dies first, unless it is transferred to joint tenancy ownership by both, or is placed in a living trust.

Joint Tenancy

Couples often own their home as "joint tenants," which means that each owns an undivided half interest in the property, and that this interest automatically passes to the other if one dies. This is called the "right of survivorship." This right is the main element that distinguishes joint tenancy from other forms of co-ownership. No post-death administrative chores are required, since joint tenancy presumes that two or more people own a whole piece of property together. The surviving joint tenant may immediately use and enjoy the property that was held in joint tenancy, for example, the family home.

Some states recognize a special form of joint tenancy, called "tenancy by the entireties," which is limited to husband and wife. Generally, however, any two or more people may own property together as joint tenants. Sometimes unmarried domestic partners, parents and children, business partners, or other groups of people set up mutual ownership in joint tenancy to achieve various purposes.

Despite its many advantages, joint tenancy is not the right form of ownership for everyone. If, for example, you wish to leave an interest in the property to someone other than your co-owners, you need to set up a different kind of ownership. Also, when property passes outside a will that tries to transfer the same property, this can disrupt an estate plan. If a couple has created a bypass trust (discussed in the next chapter), it may be better to transfer property into the trust rather than holding it as joint tenants, again depending upon the individual's circumstances. It is always best to check with an attorney first. It is essential that all the components of property ownership and estate planning work in harmony—another reason expert advice and periodic reviews of your estate plan are crucial.

Other Forms of Co-Ownership

Joint tenancy is not the only way two or more people may share ownership of property. Other forms of co-ownership, such as tenancy in common, are often used when the owners do not want the property to be subject to the automatic right of survivorship of joint tenancy ownership. These various forms of ownership affect other legal rights as well, so it is important to understand the differences between them in order to make the best choice.

For any co-owned property that is not held in joint tenancy, it is a good idea to specify on the deed or title, or in a separate written agreement, how much each person owns. Such agreements may also provide restrictions or guidelines for what should happen if one person wishes to sell her share, such as a right of first refusal, which gives co-owners the first opportunity to buy the share. These agreements are usually simple, short contracts that can be prepared by an attorney for a small fee.

Alternative Ways to Help Your Beneficiaries

In addition to designating others to receive your property as beneficiaries or co-owners after your death, there are other alternatives that should not be overlooked. For example, an estate planning document may forgive a debt. Two or more recipients may also be designated to share a gift, although this may give rise to difficult situations. For example, parents sometimes leave a family home to be shared by two or more children. This might be a great idea, or a disastrous one, depending upon each situation.

Also, you may wish to name alternative beneficiaries in case one is unable or unwilling to accept your bequest. This can be an especially important step to take if you wish to make bequests that have conditions attached, for example, a farm or business which needs a great deal of work and attention if it is to continue to operate.

For those with substantial assets, a charitable-giving plan that provides a flow of income during a beneficiary's lifetime may be a means of satisfying several goals, including charitable giving, current and future tax advantages, and helping a beneficiary. These plans are described in the next chapter.

Chapter 7

Estate Taxes, Tax-Reducing Trusts, and Gifts

Different people require different types of estate plans that will protect their property while they are alive, and to ensure that the estate will be handled as they wish after their death. To determine which methods will most effectively accomplish these goals, it is important to understand what you own and how you want it to be managed and distributed.

For most people, even planning for the disposition of a simple estate requires financial, tax, medical, and business planning, in addition to the preparation of a will, trust, or other document. For those with substantial assets, any additional issues may be involved.

Tax planning is an important component of many estate plans. Estate planning usually focuses upon federal estate (death) taxes. But other taxes, such as income, gift, real estate, or qualified retirement-plan taxes, may also be involved.

ESTATE TAXES

According to California estate attorney and author Mark J. Welch, although only about 8 percent of all estates in America owe any estate taxes, these estate taxes generate a whopping 1 percent of the entire federal revenue. While more than fifty bills to alter estate and gift taxes were introduced in Congress during the 1997 session alone, Welch notes, such bills have historically died in committees because no one could come up with a way to offset the lost tax revenue if estate taxes were eliminated or substantially reduced.

At last, however, one important reform was enacted. Under current federal tax law, only estates with a total value of $650,000 or more are subject to federal estate taxes. Estates with a lesser value are exempt from this tax. In 2000, the exempt amount increases to $675,000; in 2002 to $700,000; in 2004 to $850,000; in 2005 to $950,000; and in 2006 to $1,000,000.

Federal estate taxes are levied at rates of 37 to 55 percent, depending upon the fair-market value of the estate. This is another reason it is essential to get the full picture of the fair-market value of your assets. Many people own real estate, antiques, jewelry, or family heirlooms that appreciate in value over the years and may be worth far more than they realize. While $650,000 sounds like a great deal of money, the value of an estate, especially one that includes real estate and life insurance, can quickly add up. Many small family businesses or farms have a market value that exceeds this amount. Be sure you know the total value of your estate, so that if it is likely to be greater than the exempt amount, you can take steps to protect it.

Other Death Taxes

In addition to the federal estate taxes, your estate may be subject to other taxes that will be levied against it upon your death. About half the states have "inheritance taxes" that tax those who receive a deceased person's property. In reality, these taxes are generally paid out of the deceased person's estate.

Federal estates taxes, collected by the IRS, are administered by federal law, so they do not vary from state to state. However, probate fees and inheritance taxes vary by state, so make sure you know whether your estate may be subject to these costs as well.

HOW MUCH IS YOUR ESTATE WORTH TODAY?

Your taxable estate includes the total of the net value of your estate, plus nonexempt gifts you completed during your lifetime, less any gift tax you paid. The gross value of your estate is determined by calculating the gross value of everything you own at the time of your death, such as your home and other real estate, investments, any interest you have in a business, personal property, share of a pension plan, and a 50-percent share of any community property you own with your spouse. Benefits paid from life insurance *do* count in calculating your estate's total value. The beneficiary (for instance, your surviving spouse) won't have to pay income tax on life insurance benefits, but if your estate exceeds the exempt amount, estate taxes are charged against the total, including life insurance.

To calculate your net estate, subtract from this total any debts you or your estate owes, income taxes paid by the estate on its own income (such as income from a continuing business), the expenses of settling the estate, bequests to your spouse, and bequests to charities.

Understanding the "Basis" for Estate and Capital-Gains Taxes

In calculating the value of your estate to determine whether it may be subject to taxation, it is important to understand the concept of *basis*. For most pieces of property we hold during our lifetime, the "basis" refers to the original cost. Thus, in calculating capital-gains tax, which is charged against the "gain" a person has when selling an appreciated asset, the taxable gain is determined by the difference between the selling price today and the asset's basis, or original cost. For example, if you bought a home for $20,000 and sold it several years later for $30,000, your taxable capital gain would be $10,000. (Note that there are some exemptions available to homeowners. This is merely an example of how the capital gain is calculated.)

However, your estate's basis for an asset is calculated at its fair-market value on the date of your death. Your estate won't be required to pay capital-gains tax, but the same type of gain is figured into the total value of your estate (for example, that house now worth $30,000).

The concept of basis may be significant to you and, in the future, your heirs in different ways. First, if you own something such as a business or a piece of real estate that has appreciated in value during your lifetime, the basis—the fair-market value—calculated at your death could push an estate not otherwise subject to estate taxation over the exempt amount. It is important to know what your estate is worth today and what it is likely to be worth at the time of your death—to the extent this can be calculated—in order to determine whether it may be subject to estate taxation. Second, basis can help you and your heirs avoid capital-gains tax when an asset is sold. This is an important consideration in deciding whether to make an inter vivos gift, or to leave a particular piece of property in your estate. For example, if you have a highly appreciated asset, such as a home or other building, that you wish to give to your prospective heirs late in your life, it may be better to pass it through your estate. This way the basis is set at the fair-market value at the time of your death when your heirs receive it. So this might be the best way to transfer this asset *if* your total estate is not sufficient to trigger federal estate taxes. Thus, if your beneficiaries decide to sell the property after you are gone, it is generally subject to far lower capital gains tax.

The decision to sell or give away a highly appreciated asset—thus subjecting it to capital gains tax—or to pass it through your estate depends on many factors. They include your estate's total value and whether it will be subject to taxation, and your reasons for wishing to sell or give away the property during your lifetime. (For example, you need the money from the sale of a home to pay your present expenses when you move to a retirement community, so this will be your priority.) Again, seek the advice of a qualified professional, including an estate planning attorney and a tax accountant, if you need to make a decision in this area.

As a part of your estate planning process, it may be worthwhile to have certain pieces of your property appraised, if you suspect they may have greatly appreciated. The general rule is that an asset's value for gift, estate, and generation-skipping tax is its fair market value, defined as the agreed price between a willing buyer and a willing seller, neither being under any compulsion to buy or sell, and both having a reasonable knowledge of all relevant facts. Not surprisingly, this value is sometimes a subject of tremendous disagreement between estate representatives and IRS agents. Occasionally, these disputes over value end up in tax court, with the IRS enjoying a presumption that its valuation is correct. The burden of proof is on the estate. Should this type of conflict arise, reports from neutral appraisers can be very helpful.

Also, consider that if many years pass between the time of the appraisal and your death, the value will likely have changed. If you have assets that are especially unusual or valuable, it may be a good idea to have a new appraisal done from time to time, both for estate planning and insurance purposes, so that you will be sure that the value of the property is adequately insured while you are living.

A number of legal methods can be used to "devalue" or reduce the fair-market value of certain assets, reducing the basis of your estate. For instance, your estate may elect an alternative valuation date of six months after your death. However, when the primary concern is reducing the value of the taxable estate, certain steps can be taken to make an asset less attractive to potential buyers, without altering its actual value to you or your beneficiaries. One such option is creating a family limited partnership.

Family Limited Partnerships

A family limited partnership, if properly structured, can be a fairly easy way to shrink the fair-market value of the assets held in the partnership, thus reducing your taxable value, for purposes of making tax-exempt gifts or to your estate's total value when you die. Often, the person who creates the partnership remains general partner and controls the assets and distributions to other partners. The general partner can give a limited partnership interest, either all at once or incrementally, directly or in trust.

One reason assets held in a family limited partnership experience a reduction in their fair-market value is that in a carefully structured partnership agreement, partnership interests may not be transferred except with the consent of the general partner and a majority of limited partners; each partner holds a right of first refusal to purchase any partnership interest offered for sale by another partner. This may substantially reduce the market value of partnership assets, because such provisions make it less desirable for an outsider to own the partnership interest that is subject to these limitations.

To protect the family limited partnership, for estate tax purposes, the agreement should provide for appointment of a new general partner after your death, or when otherwise needed. This person can be named in the partnership agreement, or may be elected by the limited partners. This is important, because the partnership must be able to continue after your death in order to provide estate tax protection.

Family limited partnerships must be structured carefully by someone qualified and experienced in working with these entities. Many scams have been perpetuated by people who claim that family limited partnerships can result in total avoidance of estate taxes, as well as grandiose claims that are not true. If you are interested in a family limited partnership, work with reputable professionals in completing the necessary steps.

IRREVOCABLE TRUSTS

Most of the trusts that can be established to achieve estate tax advantages are "irrevocable trusts." These are different from the revocable living trusts discussed in the previous chapter. A revocable trust may be canceled or amended at anytime, and the assets placed in such a trust remain under the control of the person who creates it. Irrevocable trusts are independent legal entities that cannot be modified or manipulated by the maker. These trusts are often included within a living trust, and are referred to as "subtrusts" when structured in this fashion.

Any irrevocable trust should be set up carefully, because of its permanent nature, and also because of certain requirements, such as the need for a federal taxpayer identification number, and separate financial records. Trust-income tax returns must also be filed and paid each year. Yet, because they can provide substantial tax benefits, both in the present and for the estate's future, it is well worth the time and cost required to investigate and establish these trusts if you would otherwise be subject to estate taxes.

BYPASS TRUSTS FOR MARRIED COUPLES

The most common type of irrevocable trust used to save estate taxes is called a "bypass trust," "marital-shelter trust," an "A-B trust" or a "credit-shelter trust." I will refer to this type of trust here as a "bypass trust."

According to federal estate tax law, husbands and wives who leave estates to each other are not subject to the $650,000 limit (as of 1999, scheduled to increase incrementally until 2006). The "marital deduction" allows you to leave your spouse any amount of property without paying estate taxes. For example, if you own a business worth $1 million as your own separate property, and it goes to your spouse when you die, there is no estate tax as long as your spouse is a U.S. citizen. Additionally, you can pass on $650,000 to your beneficiaries, which is your federal estate tax "credit shelter" exemption.

But it is important for couples to understand that the marital deduction, which allows one spouse to will as much property as he chooses to his wife without being subject to any estate tax, does not protect the estate when the wife dies. If, for example, the husband dies first and a simple will passes his entire estate to the wife, whatever she does not spend will be included in her estate when she dies. Unless they have set up a bypass trust, only $650,000 will be sheltered from taxes.

A properly structured bypass trust can reduce, or, with smaller estates, eliminate entirely estate taxes that would otherwise have to be paid when the second spouse died. Any couple with combined assets of more than $650,000 (in 1999) should seriously consider establishing a bypass trust to protect those assets from the astronomical estate taxes that could otherwise be imposed when the second spouse dies. By using this type of trust, couples can protect assets valued at double the current federal estate tax exemption—in 1999, this means a total estate of $1.3 million.

Couples should be sure to have their bypass trust prepared professionally, because the issues involved may be complex and a great deal of money may be at stake. A bypass trust can save more than $200,000 in estate taxes, for example, on an estate with a total value of about $1.3 million, but only if it is done right. Otherwise, unless a bypass trust is correctly prepared, only $650,000 is sheltered. And on an estate with a total value of $1.3 million, more than $200,000 would be levied in estate taxes.

This exemption works in a fairly straightforward manner. When a couple sets up a bypass trust while both spouses are still alive, the income that exceeds the taxable amount—$650,000 in 1999—is placed in the bypass trust. When the first spouse dies, for example, the husband, this property is not part of his estate. The surviving spouse may draw income or principal out of the trust as needed, and as long as she doesn't add so much to the total value of her estate that it exceeds the $650,000 exempt amount when she dies, neither her estate nor the property held in trust will be subject to estate taxes.

Preparing a bypass trust is not as complicated as it may sound. A bypass trust can be included in either a will or a living trust. Depending upon the complexity of the estate, it should not cost more than a few thousand dollars, at most, for an attorney to complete all the work and documents to create the trust. When you consider that this can result in a savings of as much as $200,000 in estate taxes, it is well worth the investment.

Anyone interested in creating a bypass trust should be certain to work with a qualified legal professional. So many factors have to be considered, and it is easy to overlook something relatively simple, which can invalidate the whole plan. For example, if someone has a life insurance policy that designates his spouse as the beneficiary, the proceeds are usually a part of the taxable estate, unless he has taken the steps to create a life insurance trust. Many people are confused, because the person who receives life insurance proceeds does not have to pay income tax on these funds. However, life insurance proceeds are subject to estate tax against the estate of the person who died. So it may be important to change beneficiaries on life insurance, retirement plans, or other assets with beneficiary designations, or to set up a separate life insurance trust. This should always be done with the assistance of a professional who understands how to achieve the client's goals.

Establishing an effective bypass trust may also require that a couple change the way they own certain property, such as homes held in joint tenancy. When property is held in joint tenancy, the proceeds do not go into the bypass trust when one joint tenant dies but directly to the other joint tenant. For some couples, it is better to deed this property into the trust. This is an individual decision that must be made after reviewing the couple's assets and their situation. It depends on what they own and where they live. It is easier to set up a bypass trust in community property states. In other states, it is essential to look at the asset structure and be sure the proper amounts and kinds of assets are included in the trust. The couple may need to put certain assets into another form of ownership before the trust is created. This adds complexity, but it is absolutely essential if the desired tax savings are to be achieved.

Once this analysis of a couple's goals, property, and required steps is completed, the actual mechanics of creating the trust is generally not too difficult. For those with larger estates or special circumstances, more than one trust may be needed to achieve the goal of protecting the value of the estate for future beneficiaries. For example, the marital deduction for estate tax does not apply to property left to someone who is not an American citizen. A citizen married to a noncitizen must establish a special type of trust called a QDOT trust, which enables the noncitizen spouse to postpone payment of taxes due until after his or her death. This is important when a citizen and noncitizen couple share assets worth an amount that exceeds the federal-estate tax exemption.

Unmarried couples should also take special care to be sure that their property ownership and other components of their estate plan are carefully crafted, so that their wishes may be carried out and legally enforced. Some attorneys specialize in assisting such couples, as discussed later in the book.

QTIP Trusts

A Qualified Terminable Interest Property (QTIP) trust protects estates whose value requires more than the standard bypass trust. QTIP trusts allow a couple to delay the payment of any estate taxes until the second spouse dies, no matter how much money is in the estate. It lets the surviving spouse use trust assets for her lifetime, and receive income from the trust property. A QTIP trust, depending on how it is structured, may also allow the surviving spouse to reach, use, and spend the trust principal for her benefit during her lifetime.

If you wish to bequeath income-generating property, such as a business or rental property, to your spouse, it may be especially important to take special steps to protect this interest through a QTIP trust. If you leave your husband or wife this type of property in the form of a terminable interest, which provides that someone else (such as your children) will eventually receive the income-generating property, the bequest will not qualify for the marital deduction unless you set up a QTIP trust.

Establishing this type of trust is not difficult, but requires close attention to the legal details. The law provides that property held in trust qualifies as a QTIP if, first, your spouse, and only your spouse, will have the right to receive all the income or a fixed portion of the value of the property held in trust each year; and, second, that no one else can receive distributions as long as your spouse is still alive. Again, the steps required to establish a QTIP trust must be correctly performed if the intended purpose is to be served, so be sure you seek the assistance of a qualified professional.

OTHER TYPES OF TRUSTS COMMONLY USED IN ESTATE PLANNING

Depending upon your individual, family, and business circumstances, an estate planning attorney or financial professional may suggest other types of trusts to achieve your estate planning goals. These may include insurance trusts, annuity trusts, family land preservation trusts, and many others. A special trust may be established for the benefit of a minor child, or a disabled, or incapacitated person. Trusts may also be set up to benefit a charity. Specific types of trusts, such as offshore-investment trusts, are appropriate in particular circumstances. A general overview of some of these trusts follows.

Generation Skipping Trusts

Generation Skipping Trusts (GST) are often used by families who have substantial assets they wish to distribute among their grandchildren. These trusts place property in trust for the grandchildren of the trust maker, and thereby avoid having estate taxes charged on the trust property when the children of the trust maker die. By using a GST, grandparents can transfer up to a million dollars to their grandchildren free of estate taxes.

GSTs are set up so that the assets are actually placed in trust for the grantor's children, but the children may only use the income generated by the trust. When the children die, the principal in the trust passes tax-free to their children—the trustor's grandchildren.

Life Insurance Trusts

A common type of estate planning trust is an Irrevocable Life Insurance Trust (ILIT). The trustee holds title to a life insurance policy, and on the death of the insured, receives, manages, and distributes the policy's proceeds.

If properly created and managed, the proceeds of a life insurance policy held in trust won't be subject to federal estate taxes. Since the trust owns the policy, the insurance that is paid when you die is not a part of your estate for tax purposes. ILITs are sometimes the best way to ensure substantial savings on estates taxes. However, these trusts must be prepared carefully, and are not right for everyone.

Property Control Trusts

Different types of property control trusts can be established to accomplish specific purposes with the property you will leave after your death. They are often created as subtrusts within a living trust. For example, trusts can be established to provide for balancing the interests and needs of your spouse and your children from a former marriage. Sometimes these objectives can be accomplished without a formal trust, for example, by deeding real estate to your spouse as a "life estate." A life estate allows a person to use and enjoy the benefit of a home or other property for the duration of his life, then provides that the property will be received by another person upon the death of the individual who holds the life estate. Yet a trust can achieve this objective while providing other benefits as well.

Many life estate trusts or other arrangements are set up so that the person who will enjoy use of the property during their lifetime is not allowed to sell it or otherwise change its character or affect its value. For example, a wife may place a home she owns in trust for her surviving husband to use during his lifetime, then upon his death (or in some cases, his remarriage), title in the home passes to her children. The husband may be allowed to live in the home or to rent it and use the income, but may not sell it or borrow against it.

Trusts to Provide for Children

Various trusts can be set up to provide for the needs of your children. Since minors cannot legally own large sums of money, it is important to create an appropriate trust, and to name a competent trustee, if you have a substantial estate and young children. Such trusts may be established for each child, or all children can be covered by one trust (which is often easier). This is called a "family pot trust" or "sprinkling trust." A single trustee can use the assets in the trust to provide for each child, as needed. Many parents include such trusts as subtrusts in their living trusts or wills, so that if they both die before their children are adults, their assets will be managed for the children according to the individual circumstances of each child, as they may change (for example, if one child shows a special aptitude for music and needs lessons, while another suffers an illness and incurs medical bills).

Individual trusts can also be set up for each child. This is sometimes the best decision, depending, as always, on individual circumstances. Establishing any trust for a child requires a great deal of forethought, careful choice of one or more trustees, and expert assistance.

Most of the trusts established for children are some species of property controlled trusts. Trusts may be established to help pay for a child's college or other schooling costs, or to care for a person with special needs, for example, someone who is disabled. Some restrict a beneficiary's access to her inheritance under a "spendthrift trust," or provide conditions the person must meet to receive the funds. I recall one such trust that required the beneficiary to be employed or enrolled as a full-time student to ensure that she didn't simply loll around living off the trust income.

Parents may also provide for their minor children by creating a custodial account according to the requirements of the Uniform Transfer to Minors Act (UTMA), which has been adopted by most states. Under this law, a parent may include a clause in her will stating that she is making certain bequests pursuant to the Uniform Transfers to Minors Act. She then states the amount of the gift, names a custodian (and an alternate custodian in case the first person named is not able to fulfill his duties). If the parent dies, then the custodian will have broad discretion to use the property for the child's benefit, and will not have to make annual reports or deal with other requirements of court supervision, as would a property guardian. Of course, some parents prefer to have the additional protection of court supervision, and if this is the case, then it is preferable to take the traditional route of appointing a property guardian.

By using UTMA or another law, the Uniform Gifts to Minors Act (UGMA, also adopted by most states), parents can also establish a custodial trust account for their minor children while they are still living. Doing so may provide current tax benefits, as well as reducing the size of the parents' estate for estate tax planning purposes. Parents retain control of the funds transferred under UTMA or UGMA by naming themselves custodians until the child reaches majority (eighteen or twenty-one, depending on the state). A successor custodian trustee is named to manage the account in case the parents die while the child is still a minor.

Any gift made under UTMA or UGMA is subject to the same gift tax provisions as any other gift; that is, if more than $10,000 is gifted to any one individual each year it will be taxed (as discussed below). But once the property is placed in this type of trust account, if the child is over thirteen, then the income it generates is taxed to the child, at a rate far lower than the parent would be required to pay. Such an account should always be established with the assistance of a tax or legal adviser, to be certain that it achieves the intended goals.

INTER VIVOS GIFTS

As we've explained, many people simplify their estate planning by giving away part of their property during their lifetime (referred to in the law as "inter vivos" gifts). This can be a shrewd move that serves several purposes, including: avoiding or reducing estate taxes; ensuring that your property goes to those you wish to receive it; and increasing your eligibility for government assistance if you should become incapacitated by age or illness.

Inter vivos gifts may also provide a tax benefit during your lifetime.

According to gift tax laws, any person may give any other person a gift with a total value of $10,000 in one year without being subject to a gift tax. According to recent changes in the federal tax laws, this amount will likely increase by 2001, although whether this will actually occur, and the amount of the increase remains uncertain, so be sure to check with a tax professional if you need current information. As this book is being written in 1999, the credit remains $10,000, so we will stay with that figure.

If you wish to distribute your estate among different individuals, wisely planned inter vivos gift-giving can transfer much more than $10,000 per year. Annual exempt gifts to family members or others of up to $10,000 per year *per recipient* can be made without being subject to tax. Therefore, two parents of four children may transfer $10,000 to each of the four children every year. If the children are married and the gift is made to the child and his spouse, the gift may reach a value of $20,000, since $10,000 may be given to each individual. Therefore, if each of their four children is married, our hypothetical parents could transfer up to $80,000 per year in assets to their children and sons- and daughters-in-law.

Or, a man who owns a house valued at $50,000, for example, may transfer the deed to the home to his daughter, and then take back a mortgage on the property. For each of the five years following the transfer, he can "forgive" $10,000 owed on the mortgage. At the end of five years, title to the house is legally vested in the daughter, and the father has avoided the gift tax because he actually gave his daughter only $10,000 per year.

One word of caution, however: In calculating federal estate taxes, the value of any *nonexempt gift* completed during the giver's lifetime, minus any paid gift tax, is included in the total value of his estate when he dies, in order to calculate estate taxes. Therefore, if you plan to give someone a gift worth more than $10,000, speak with a tax accountant or other adviser to gain a clear understanding of how the gift could impact upon your present gift-tax obligations, as well as your future estate-tax burden.

If these concerns are addressed and inter vivos giving is carefully planned, it can be the best way to transfer certain types of assets. For example, during the 1960s and 1970s, the value of farm land skyrocketed in many parts of the country. Family farms that had been handed down to the generation of current owners before estate taxes existed were now subject to devastating taxation. Combined with other factors that made life increasingly hard for family farmers, estate taxes sometimes resulted in the loss of a farm property when the last spouse died. Many farm owners began transferring a few acres a year to their children or other beneficiaries as a means of avoiding the tax crunch. Under similar circumstances, inter vivos giving—sometimes combined with bypass trusts or other tools—may prove to be the best way to effect such a transfer.

In addition to the $10,000 annual exemption for gifts, other tax exemptions may apply in certain circumstances. Gifts made to your spouse or a charitable organization, tuition paid directly to a student's school, or medical expenses paid directly to a patient's doctor or hospital are generally exempt from gift tax—with some limitations. Gifts to charities and other qualified nonprofit organizations can also provide a present income-tax deduction. Also, a gift that is considered "incomplete" under the law is not taxable. If you retain the right to have the property eventually returned to you or the right to name other people to share in the gift—along with certain other exceptions for stock or life insurance—the gift is not complete and not subject to tax. (Charitable giving plans are discussed in more detail below.)

Emotional Advantages of Inter Vivos Giving

Aside from the potential tax advantages, giving away property while you are still alive can help make things easier for both the giver and the recipient rather than transferring property through your estate. Some years ago, one of my aunts began regularly urging her relatives to speak up about which pieces of her property they would like to have when she died. Her estate plan was simple and complete, leaving everything to her only child, but she wanted to distribute a few special heirlooms among her nieces, nephews, and grandchildren. Although she handled the issue with her customary humor—albeit, black humor—the thought of contemplating her death by accepting these gifts made me squirm mightily. For a while, I resisted claiming anything, but then I realized it would make her happy, as well as contribute to her peace of mind if I accepted a few items I had always been fond of. The process also helped her clear some clutter from her home and cut down on housekeeping chores as she grew older. I finally put my own discomfort aside and accepted a few things she urged me to take. While she was still alive, I was able to assure her that I did use and enjoy these things, which pleased her. When she died in her mid eighties, the task of sorting through what remained was made easier on her son and the rest of her family, because she had already distributed a good deal of her property.

In contrast, I have seen families in which the children started bickering over the antiques—even going so far as to start tagging with their names what they wanted—when their parents were still healthy, working, and not yet sixty years old! While such blatant grasping horrified me, these parents laughed it off and even encouraged the children to battle it out, so they would know how to designate who would receive each item of property as they completed their estate plan.

Other families arrange a meeting or weekend retreat in which everyone is urged (or in some cases, forced) to sit down and face the issue of family estate planning, no matter how difficult it may be.

While such efforts may be emotionally wrenching, especially for those of us who would like to believe that our loved ones can live forever, they can impart a great deal of peace of mind, and perhaps even more importantly, avoid disputes that amplify the pain of a parent's or other loved one's death. These disputes are always a miserable ordeal, whether they amount to no more than a teary argument over who gets grandmother's silver tea service, or a full-blown courtroom battle. Families have been torn apart for years by the bitterness resulting from even the most petty disputes over a small, but emotionally charged, piece of property. Therefore, it is best to get as many people involved and as many questions and plans resolved as is humanly possible, for both the practical and emotional aspects of creating your estate plan.

CHARITABLE GIFTS AND TRUSTS

Charitable gifts and trusts can be a beneficial tool for anyone who wishes to make a large gift to a charitable organization, both for income-tax savings during life and estate-tax benefits after death. A charitable trust may be a smart move even for those whose estates are not large enough to trigger federal estate taxes.

Christopher M. O'Neill, Ph.D., is a financial planner and investment adviser representative who offers financial planning services through W. S. Griffith and Co., Inc., a registered investment adviser in Albuquerque, New Mexico. Dr. O'Neill specializes in helping clients to build, protect, and preserve their net worth. "One important component of protecting assets is the application of wise estate planning techniques," he states. "We try to recommend courses of action aimed at minimizing taxes and maintaining the amount of the estate that will pass to the client's beneficiaries. Gifts to charity during one's lifetime or at death can reduce the size of the taxable estate, as well as provide a current income tax deduction in most cases."

To achieve these goals for clients with different assets and needs, O'Neill uses a collection of varied charitable-giving techniques. "For some people, the best method is simply to make an outright gift to a nonprofit or other charitable organization," he explains. "For others, however, such a direct gift is not feasible, and they require more sophisticated giving techniques."

Numerous methods can be used to enable a person with a charitable intent, but for whom a one time gift is not the best option, to benefit a chosen charity while at the same time enjoy tax and other estate planning advantages. "Many options are available for those who are not able to contribute the entire asset during their lifetime. These methods can enhance the benefits of charitable giving," he remarks.

The most important point in determining whether this type of plan may be appropriate for a particular individual is whether the person has a sincere charitable intent. "The motivation to give is the starting point," O'Neill says. "The underlying meaning is very important, because these tools are more than just financial planning filters. Often, the result is irrevocable, so one needs to be clear about the motivation."

While most charitable giving plans require a certain level of wealth, even people who do not presently have an estate large enough to be subject to estate taxes may find such tools meaningful, O'Neill maintains. "There are also current income-tax benefits," he explains. "It all depends on the individual's motivations and circumstances, as well as the technique."

Onetime Gifts

O'Neill points out that there are trade-offs involved in employing the more sophisticated giving techniques, as opposed to making a straightforward gift to charity. "Most of the more complex charitable plans require payment of professional fees to set up the trust or other plan, and some also involve ongoing management expenses," he explains. "For those below a certain net-worth level, it may be better to give an outright gift. But it really depends on each person's situation and desires."

Life Insurance Charitable Plans

One of the simplest ways for an individual, especially a person with modest assets, to fulfill a desire to benefit a charitable organization and achieve tax benefits is through the use of a life insurance charitable plan, O'Neill explains. "If the alternative is between a relatively small one time gift and a technique that will provide both the giver and the charity greater benefits in the long run, a life insurance charitable plan may be one viable option," he states. "This can involve the transfer of an existing policy as an outright gift to the charity, or a plan in which the donor contributes funds, so the charity buys the policy of insurance on the donor's life. The charity will receive a large sum in the future. This can be a great technique for someone who has a certain amount of income they wish to set aside for a charitable purpose."

A life insurance charitable plan can provide both income tax benefits and estate tax advantages. "It may amount to an initial gift, as well as an ongoing gift," O'Neill explains. "In either case, the initial transfer provides an income tax deduction, and any additional contributions to pay annual premiums on the policy are also tax-deductible. Then the life insurance, an asset that would have been subject to estate tax, is removed from your estate, which reduces the value of the estate."

Establishing a life insurance plan is simpler and less expensive than most of the other sophisticated charitable-giving techniques, O'Neill emphasizes. "It's the most down- to-earth and accessible of the advanced techniques. There is no trust to be established, so there isn't a great deal of legal work to be done. It simply involves making a gift of life insurance and/or subsequent premiums to charity. Because the charity is the owner, it enjoys all the incidents of ownership, of a living asset with present benefits. This technique significantly benefits the charity."

This type of plan may be especially appropriate for an older person who purchased life insurance to provide replacement income for a family that no longer needs or expects the same level of protection, and for whom income and estate taxes now pose a greater concern. But O'Neill cautions that even with this simpler form of giving, many fine points should be considered, as should be the potential downsides for certain individuals. "Certain requirements must be met to qualify for the income-tax deduction," he notes. "Work with a financial adviser who understands the requirements and consequences of the various charitable-giving techniques." O'Neill adds that a life insurance charitable plan is different from an irrevocable life insurance trust, which is discussed below.

Split-Interest Gifts

For those who are not in a position to contribute a onetime gift of an entire asset, a split-interest deferred gift may be the answer. With this technique, the ownership interest in the asset is divided, with one portion given in trust for the charity, while another portion—often income from the asset—is retained by the donor.

In addition to income tax deductions for the value of the gift, these contributions also reduce the gross value of the taxable estate. This results in estate tax savings, because ownership of the donated asset has either already passed to the charity or will pass as a remainder interest from the trust to the charity when the owner (or other named beneficiary) dies. In many cases, capital-gains taxes are also saved because an asset that has appreciated over the years the donor owned it (for example, a parcel of real estate bought for $25,000 that is now worth

$250,000) is instead donated and turned into an income-producing asset by the charity.

A split interest gift can address a common problem that may arise when a substantial portion of a person's estate is given to charity: Children or others who expected to inherit the property may be hurt or angry. "One way to soften the blow is by using one of the income-producing trusts, with the heir designated as beneficiary, to replace the asset," O'Neill explains. "This can be especially beneficial to the heirs if an asset that is not currently deriving income and would result in a huge estate tax bill—such as a large parcel of highly appreciated land—can be converted into something that produces income now."

An irrevocable life insurance trust can also be used to complement this approach by replacing the asset gifted to charity. "Land can be traded, in effect, for life insurance paid for by part of the income generated by the gift," O'Neill explains. "This saves estate taxes and provides extra income, while ultimately benefitting a charitable organization."

Charitable Remainder Trusts

When the donor gives a split-interest gift in which he retains the right to receive income from the asset but transfers his rights in the "remainder"—final ownership of the asset itself—to a charity or charitable trust, it is called a charitable remainder trust. Several species of charitable remainder trusts are described below, from the least complex to the most sophisticated.

Charitable Gift Annuities

For clients who have fairly substantial assets yet do not wish to give an outright gift, a Charitable Gift Annuity (CGA) may be the best tool. "This technique provides an ongoing benefit to the organization, as well as returning an income stream to the donor," O'Neill explains. "The donor transfers the asset directly to the charity in exchange for the charity's agreement to pay a lifetime annuity. It's fairly simple to arrange, and it provides an initial, one time income tax deduction for the gift. But a CGA still allows the donor, or any other designated beneficiary, to receive a fixed-dollar amount, set at the time the gift is made, each year for the rest of the giver's life."

Pooled Income Fund

A pooled income fund also provides the giver with returned income on the donated assets but requires a pool of funds contributed by many different donors. "Colleges often establish pooled income funds," O'Neill notes. "This type of giving provides both income tax and estate tax benefits, and it's not terribly complex. You can participate in such structures without a lot of bells and whistles, yet they allow you to get more out of your gift."

In a pooled income fund, the donor transfers an asset to a fund maintained by the charity. The charity owns this asset outright as part of a common investment fund. "The charity's trustee is responsibile for paying the donor a percentage share of the fund's annual income, calculated in proportion to the value of the contributed asset," O'Neill explains. "Payments continue for the life of the donor and his spouse, and may increase or decrease according to the fund's investment performance."

As with other charitable-gift plans, the donor may specify that this income be paid to another beneficiary, but he should be careful to check on the possible gift tax consequences if the beneficiary receives more than $10,000 per year. When the donor or other named beneficiary dies, the remaining assets pass to the charity.

Charitable Remainder Unitrusts and Annuity Trusts

Moving to the more complicated charitable giving techniques, O'Neill explains that certain remainder trusts hold advantages for clients for whom these tools are appropriate. "These trusts can be customized a little more within their set parameters," he explains. "They come in different 'flavors'—each involving an income stream and a remainder—a future interest that is owned by a trust during the donor's lifetime and which is then transferred to the charity. In this situation, the trust is irrevocable, and while the charity doesn't receive an immediate benefit, it will gain full ownership of a valuable asset after the giver's death." Remainder trusts are not for everyone, O'Neill warns, and complex calculations are required to determine income and tax characteristics of a given arrangement.

Charitable Remainder Unitrusts The flexibility of these trusts allows the donor to obtain greater benefits. "For example, with a Charitable Remainder Unitrust—or CRUT—a person who owns a highly appreciated asset, such as land or stock that has skyrocketed in value, can avoid the capital gains tax that would be charged if it was sold outright, by putting it into one of these. The trust sells the asset (and it does not have to pay capital gains tax), and then invests the proceeds into other income-producing assets. The donor retains the right to receive a certain percentage of the income from the trust. If the value of the asset continues to grow, so will the income," O'Neill explains.

Charitable Remainder Annuity Trusts A Charitable Remainder Annuity Trust—or CRAT—is similar to a CRUT, but pays a fixed-dollar annuity year after year. In either case, the donor is still collecting asset income that might not have been available if the asset were still in her estate, as well as benefiting charity, getting a current tax deduction, avoiding capital-gains tax, and reducing or avoiding estate taxes.

Charitable Lead Trusts

"A charitable lead trust, also called a charitable income trust, is the inverse of a Charitable Remainder Trust," O'Neill explains. "Valuable assets are still put into a trust, but the income from the assets goes to the charity. Like the charitable remainder trust, charitable lead trusts pay interest in fixed dollar amounts (charitable lead annuity trust, or CLAT) or as a percentage of the donated assets (charitable lead unitrust, or CLUT). The assets held in the trust—the remainder interest—revert to the donor or are passed on to the heirs when the trust ends. The donor is allowed to take a tax deduction on the income that is donated to the charity."

A Charitable Lead Trust may also help reduce estate taxes by taking income out of the estate. The amount of estate tax deduction, as well as how much of the trust assets are left for the heirs, depends upon several factors. These include the number of years the assets are held in trust, the percentage of income paid annually to the charity, and how well the trustee invests the assets.

A lead trust may be the right choice for those who wish to benefit charity and gain tax benefits but not give up total control or ownership of assets, and/or pass them on to heirs, O'Neill says. "Jacqueline Onassis, for example, wanted to benefit charity, but at the same time not disinherit her children. So she left her entire estate to a charitable lead trust for that purpose. The trust would make payments to charity for twenty-four years, then whatever remained in the trust would pass to her children and grandchildren. As a result, almost all of Onassis' estate, valued on the order of $100 million, should pass to her heirs free of estate tax!" O'Neill cautions that this type of trust may not provide everyone with the same estate tax benefits some of the other charitable techniques can, but serves other purposes that may be more important to the individual.

Private Family Foundations

For those with significant wealth and a strong desire to assist one or more charities, a private family foundation can allow a family to retain greater control over their donated assets. "Family foundations are the pinnacle of complexity and expense to establish and maintain, but they can be a good alternative for the wealthy person for whom continued control of their assets is important," O'Neill notes. "They are regulated in a different manner from standard charitable trusts, because they are organizations in themselves, which require officers, directors, and ongoing time and expense to run and manage. But they satisfy the goals of some families that want the flexibility and don't mind the work."

Use Caution When Dealing with Sophisticated Giving Techniques

O'Neill urges those who may have an interest in utilizing one of the more sophisticated charitable-giving techniques to educate themselves through reading and studying the available options. But he cautions that the types of generalizations often encountered in the financial press can be dangerous. "Even in respected publications like the *Wall Street Journal,* you see huge stretches," he explains. "Specific circumstances must be addressed in a precise, clear manner by a qualified professional. And bad planning can result in more than a failure to accomplish the intended purpose: it can tear families apart."

In assessing the feasibility of any of these sophisticated charitable giving techniques, it is crucial to involve expert professional advisers who are familiar with both the methods you wish to consider and your own unique financial and personal circumstances.

Once you choose to transfer assets through such a plan, you must be certain that the correct steps are taken to establish a workable, legal approach that meets your goals. For example, some of these techniques require that the applicable income tax deductions be spread over more than one year if they exceed certain percentage of income limitations. Others are subject to additional government regulations and requirements.

"It's just plain complicated," O'Neill emphasizes. "And it's not something that can be accomplished through a 'one-stop shopping' approach. Often, the role of the financial planner is to analyze a person's overall financial situation, and then bring to the table certain charitable giving techniques that seem appropriate. The best context for this is in a financial analysis and planning effort that occurs before the individual goes to an estate planning attorney. The key is to talk to someone who has a grasp of your entire financial picture."

O'Neill stresses the importance of understanding the role of a financial planner. "There is a difference between assessing the financial details and executing the legal work, which is done by attorneys," he explains. Sophisticated planning may also require the involvement of a tax accountant. "The role of a financial planner or adviser is to bring ideas to the table—then attorneys and accountants must get involved in order to realize these ideas. One sign of a professional is a person who looks to others to accomplish things that are outside the scope of his expertise. This is a matter of professional responsibility, as well as professional liability."

SPECIAL CIRCUMSTANCES AND LIFE CHANGES MAY IMPACT ESTATE PLANNING

Those who own estates with a large value, who own a business, who have been married more than once, or who have not married but live with a domestic partner, for instance, all face special estate-planning concerns that require careful crafting of a plan to ensure that their goals are achieved.

A thorough estate plan should do more than just reduce your estate's tax bill. It should also have mechanisms in place to protect the property you leave your heirs, as well as give them opportunities to avoid unnecessary tax on the income from that property. Other protections appropriate in each case include shielding the property from frivolous lawsuits.

It is also important to consider the degree to which you wish to continue to manage the assets that will eventually go to your beneficiaries. You may wish to make an outright gift to one of your children or grandchildren and set up trusts for the others.

Consider the Future When Making Gifts

Occasionally, people go too far in trying to achieve their estate planning goals. Overenthusiasm in taking such steps as giving away too much property during your lifetime can lead to hardship during your later years. As you begin to formulate your plan, consider all the contingencies, such as unforeseen expenses, a change in investment values, or other factors that might affect your ability to survive comfortably on the money you have left yourself to live on for your remaining years.

THE INDIVIDUAL OR FAMILY-OWNED BUSINESS

Small businesses now account for the majority of the commerce conducted in America. In many areas, small businesses comprise as much as 90 percent of local employment and trade. An estimated $8 trillion will change hands between twentieth-century owners of family businesses and those who will inherit from them in the next century. The family-owned business will, by all accounts, continue to be a major component in the global economic system and command a high concentration of wealth in the next century.

Entrepreneurial families must take special steps in planning for the transfer of their estates in order to preserve accumulated value in the business, and to ensure its survival. Basic issues include who will operate the business after an owner's death; how to avoid or carefully plan probate of the business as part of the estate property; and how to minimize the impact of estate and other taxes on the business.

Business estate planning is a complicated matter that requires expert assistance. A word of caution: Even those who have already done long-range planning for the future of their company may not have fully considered all of the tax consequences of anticipated transfers. Some small business owners who believe they have formulated a sound plan have not fully addressed these important tax issues. Experts say that properly planning for transfer of business ownership is every bit as important as writing a will.

Even a modest business may be valued, for tax purposes, at a sum that exceeds the estate tax exemption. However, the same business may not bring that amount—or even enough to pay the probate fees and estate taxes—on the open market if it must be sold to cover these costs. And estate taxes must be paid nine months after the date of the person's death, or penalties are assessed, which, of course, add to the bill. Cases have occurred in which, for example, a business valued at $1 million incurs probate fees and estate taxes of more than $200,000 when the owner dies. Even if the beneficiaries want to sell the business, it will not bring more than $150,000. Therefore, not only do the beneficiaries receive nothing from the sale of the business, but they also end up having to use their own assets to pay the taxes on it. This kind of fiasco can be avoided by a good estate plan that combines adequate life insurance, inter vivos giving, creation of the appropriate trusts, liquidation of assets before death, and other estate planning tools.

It may also be wise to transfer ownership of the business to a carefully structured partnership or corporation. For example, Patrick owns a shoe store outright as sole proprietor. If the store is appraised at a market value of $2 million, his estate faces potential liability of more than $700,800 in estate tax when he dies. Patrick's two sons, Liam and John, work with him in the business, and he wants them to be able to continue to run the store after he is gone. But the tax bill he now faces would almost certainly require Liam and John to sell the business simply to satisfy the tax. Depending upon the market and other unpredictable factors, the store might not even bring enough to cover the tax bill, so Liam and John would have to liquidate other assets or use their own funds to cover the taxes—and still lose the family business.

However, if Patrick transfers ownership of the store to a limited partnership, for example, he keeping a 1-percent interest for himself as general partner and transfering the other 99 percent to a trust, the estate's fair-market value may be lowered by as much as 30 percent. He has reduced the potential estate tax proportionately. The main reason for the reduction in value is the undesirability for an outside investor of owning a limited-partnership interest rather than owning the underlying investments, and therefore having no say in management. As general partner, Patrick retains his decision-making authority. In many cases, the partnership agreement prohibits the sale of the business except with the general partner's consent. The partnership could also be structured to bring Liam and John in as partners, now or later.

Different devices such as limited-liability companies or various species of limited partnerships may be used to achieve this goal, and may be combined with other steps, including generation-skipping trusts or inter vivos gifts to further whittle the estate taxes. Again, such complex estate-planning devices require the assistance of expert advisers. Partnership agreements or other documents must be carefully drafted to serve the purpose they intend, without giving rise to unintended consequences that may be detrimental during your lifetime.

Buy-Sell Agreements

One of the most common ways for a closely held business to accomplish a future transfer is through the use of a buy-sell agreement. This can arrange for a smooth transition in the event that one of the owners dies, and often provides that the purchase of the business be funded through life insurance bought for each owner. For example, if one owner dies, the buy-sell agreement may state that the insurance policy's death benefits are to be paid out to the surviving owners or directly to the business. In this way, other owners have the money they need to purchase the part of the company that was owned by the person who died. If the business is a corporation, cash is often provided to the family in exchange for the deceased owner's shares. As always, tax concerns must be addressed, and additional devices such as trusts may be required to achieve the intended results.

The buy-sell agreement should spell out in detail how the ownership transfer is to be accomplished, including the obligations of all parties involved and how the business is valued at the time of the transfer. This way, the surviving owners don't have to worry about negotiating a price when one of the owners dies. When all of these details are ironed out in the buy-sell agreement, this type of planning can help avoid disputes.

A buy-sell agreement generally takes one of two approaches. The first is known as the entity purchase, in which the company itself buys out the owner's interest when she dies. This type of plan is reasonably easy to accomplish, with the main task being for the company to buy life insurance on each shareholder and designate the business as the beneficiary. However, an entity-purchase agreement may carry hidden risks. The surviving owners may face unforeseen, and potentially major, complications, including paying a high tax bill if they decide to sell the business. In some cases, the IRS will insist that life insurance death benefits be included in the company's value. Also, if the company is a "C" Corporation, it may be taxed on the insurance proceeds under what is called an alternative minimum tax. Notably, the alternative minimum tax does not affect "S" Corporations.

The second method of creating a buy-sell agreement is called a cross-purchase agreement. Under this type of arrangement, the surviving co-owners purchase the deceased owner's interest by using the life insurance proceeds. A cross-purchase agreement usually offers the best tax advantages. One major advantage is that business owners buying out the deceased owner's interest in the company are in a better position if they decide to sell the business. Because of the way the sums are calculated, the capital-gains tax bill is smaller when the business is sold. Thus, if a company's co-owners anticipate that any of them might want to sell the business if one of the other owners dies, a cross-purchase agreement is generally preferred.

Also, entity-purchase agreements often make it easier for creditors to reach the insurance proceeds that have been earmarked for the purchase of the business. Bank loans often state that the company cannot use corporate funds to buy out a shareholder's stock when there are outstanding loans. Therefore, if the owners receive the insurance proceeds under a cross-purchase agreement, the bank doesn't have this automatic claim to the money, as it would under an entity-purchase agreement. Here, the life insurance proceeds were paid to the company rather than to the other co-owners.

Some businesses with several owners have shied away from cross-purchase agreements, because they believe that the need for each owner to purchase a life insurance policy on the life of every other owner makes the process too complicated. However, a cross-purchase agreement can be set up with a single insurance policy on the life of each owner, and a partnership among the owners. The policies are held by an escrow agent or by the partnership. When one owner dies, the escrow agent or the partnership collects the benefits, purchases the deceased owner's stock, and distributes it to the other co-owners according to the terms of the agreement. This can also reduce income tax complications.

Others hesitate to set up a buy-sell agreement because of the expense. Preparation of this type of agreement generally costs between $1,000 and $5,000, and the insurance premium must be paid as well. However, the initial cost, as well as the premium expense depends on numerous factors, including the value of the business, the age of the owners, and the amount of insurance purchased. Financial advisers say that the expense is usually justified by the peace of mind in knowing that the business will continue after their death, and that their family and co-owners won't be forced to sell the business to acquire the money to pay federal estate taxes. Experts also recommend that this type of planning should be done as early as possible, preferably when the business is started.

Like any estate plan, a buy-sell arrangement may have to be adjusted as the business evolves. Consider revamping the plan whenever the company has diversified or enjoyed substantial growth, when new owners are added or old ones leave, and when the owners' children become adults who may be brought into the business.

SPECIAL PROTECTIONS FOR THE LARGER ESTATE

For those who have estates of a total value in excess of $2 million (which, as noted, include many middle-class families who own small businesses), special steps must be taken to avoid losing a large part of the estate to federal taxes.

Chapter 6 described a variety of charitable-giving techniques that can help those with substantial assets escape a severe tax bite, while at the same time benefiting a charity or nonprofit organization. Other trusts, such as bypass trusts available to married couples, or generation-skipping trusts described in that chapter, can also help offset or delay estate taxes. For some people, however, these techniques are limited or not appropriate to their circumstances. Fortunately, other options may be available to reduce the estate tax burden and also provide present benefits.

Foreign Corporations and Offshore Trusts

U.S. citizens with substantial assets may, under the right circumstances, enjoy considerable tax benefits both during their lives and on behalf of their estate after death by establishing a foreign corporation, an offshore trust account, or some combination of entities. "An offshore corporation established in a country that is a tax haven, such as the Cayman Islands or Bermuda, can save up to 40 percent in taxes, as well as providing confidentiality and protection of assets," explains James E. Kirk, an attorney experienced in establishing such entities.

Offshore trusts and foreign corporations must be carefully structured, so that they are legal and achieve the goals the grantor desires. "You have to be careful, because there are some shady arrangements that can get you in a great deal of trouble, Kirk says. "But, if they are structured carefully and legally, these entities can be excellent tools. This is a highly specialized practice, and clients who are interested should be extremely careful to work with attorneys and/or accountants who are competent in the area."

Finding someone with the requisite expertise might require some research and travel, but the potential risks involved in an incorrectly established trust or corporation make the effort worthwhile, Kirk maintains. "There are some people posing as experts, attorneys and others, who charge exorbitant fees and give bad advice," he explains. "I have seen plans that would subject the person to a horrible gift tax or other problems."

Offshore Trusts

Despite the need for caution, several significant advantages can arise from establishing an offshore trust, and such trusts are becoming more and more common, Kirk says. "Thousands of people are now using offshore trusts. One major advantage is that if the trust is set up right, then upon the death of the grantor, no estate taxes will be owed. Unlike a foreign corporation, an offshore trust generally does not give the grantor an income tax advantage, but it can be helpful in preserving wealth after death."

People are sometimes wary of offshore trusts, because they are concerned about a loss of control over their assets, he adds. "The trust articles can be set up so that there is no loss of control; the grantor retains full control over what is done with the assets. In most foreign trusts, someone is appointed to serve as 'protector' of the assets. This person serves as an adviser to the trust. Normally, the maker of the trust fills this role. In this way, offshore trusts are similar to living trusts, whereby the maker also controls the assets. However, people should understand that offshore trusts, unlike living trusts, are irrevocable."

Offshore trusts are often favored by people who have both a high income and a substantial risk of being subjected to lawsuits, for example, physicians who may be sued for malpractice. "Many people establish offshore trusts for asset protection, as well as estate-planning purposes," he notes. "The goals of my clients seem to be about evenly split between asset protection, estate protection, and estate planning."

According to Terry Coxon, author and president of Passport Financial, Inc., an offshore trust can be the most powerful of all financial planning tools for some investors. Writing in the fall 1998 edition of *Personal Investing News,* Coxon advises that an offshore trust can mean big tax savings for you and future generations, as well as to protect accumulated wealth in the face of the current litigation explosion. This type of privacy and asset shield can be important for those who have accumulated substantial wealth that may fall prey to an unscrupulous individual eager to press a lawsuit against a "deep pocket."

Unfortunately, wholly baseless lawsuits are becoming more common in the American judicial system. While there are tools such as Federal Rule of Civil Procedure 11, and the court's contempt powers—which can be applied to deter frivolous lawsuits and impose sanctions against those who bring them—many judges are reluctant to use them. The American courts also recognize a strong interest in free access to them, so, as illustrated in the story told in the introduction, even the most idiotic claims are often allowed to proceed to the point where an estate may be drained of virtually all of its assets. For people with substantial wealth or exposure to such claims as malpractice, asset protection may be an important concern.

While the requirements of establishing a foreign trust may be complex, the cost of doing so need not be exorbitant, and, as with a bypass trust, the savings can make the expenditure well worth it, if it is done correctly. "The cost depends on the country where the trust is established," Kirk explains. "You may need to set up a foreign corporation as an adjunct to a trust. There may also be fees established by that country's government, and attorneys in both countries must be paid. But it shouldn't cost more than a few thousand dollars unless the plan is very complex."

An offshore trust should be designed by American lawyers well versed in avoiding disputes with government agencies, and it should be examined by American accountants who fully understand the reporting requirements for offshore trusts. But anyone considering a foreign trust should be prepared to travel to the country where the trust will be established, Kirk adds. "A domestic attorney can give you advice on what you need to do, and help you choose an appropriate country," he explains. "But it is generally better to let the attorneys in that country take care of the paperwork, because they are more familiar with that nation's requirements. When I set up a foreign trust for a client, I always work with a good, reputable law firm in the country concerned."

Kirk advises clients who are able to travel to the country where the trust will be set up to contact an established, reputable law firm, or go to a stable bank and speak to a bank officer about the types of trusts available. "Many banks in countries that are widely used by foreign citizens have trust departments which understand what is required," he explains.

As offshore trusts become more common and increasingly popular, greater numbers of people are seeking or providing information about them. Kirk is concerned that much of this information may be inaccurate. "Most financial planners don't know that much about foreign corporations and offshore trusts unless they specialize in the field," he cautions. "It is best to seek the advice of someone who has a solid reputation as an expert in this field. For example," he recalls, "a client recently came to me for advice about a plan someone else had set up for him. He had been charged about $5,000 by someone who created a stupid, and mostly illegal, maze. Not only did it fail to serve the purpose, but it also resulted in his loss of control over his assets, and put him into a dangerous situation in which he believes he won't have to pay any taxes at all. Unless he has this corrected by someone who knows what they are doing, he will face a nightmare someday."

Investors contemplating a foreign protective trust or corporation should work with financial advisers who are experienced and competent at setting up this particular type of trust. Some reputable firms, such as Passport Financial, conduct seminars for people interested in learning more about these topics. (Several such companies are listed in the Appendix.)

An offshore trust should be flexible, so that it may be adapted to changes in American laws, investment conditions, and the grantor's family circumstances. It should be able to hold any kind of investment, and be easy to coordinate with your other financial-planning tools, such as a living trust or a bypass trust.

An offshore trust can hold almost any type of asset, including stocks, bonds, and mutual funds traded in any U.S. or foreign market; precious metals and foreign currencies; and life insurance, annuities, and policies issued in foreign currencies. If a family business is incorporated, it may also be transferred to an offshore trust by transferring the stock; or a limited-partnership interest representing most of the business' value if it is a partnership. The owner usually retains control of the business as a corporate officer and director, or as the general partner.

An offshore trust lets you have as little or as much control over managing your investments as you choose, Coxon points out. If you have a brokerage account, you may continue to work with the investment broker of your choice, with the account registered in the name of your trust. Alternatively, the trustee can set up a new account for your trust with a broker in a foreign country. If you use a professional investment adviser, you may also move the investments into your trust but still keep the same adviser to manage them. The trustee can also be given the responsibility for managing all or a portion of the trust as a tax-management portfolio, for safety, profit, and tax savings.

During your lifetime, your offshore trust is income tax neutral, says Coxon. But a qualified trustee can help you locate tax-advantaged investments for the trust property, which are not readily available in the United States. However, it is usually your heirs who receive the greatest tax benefits.

Moreover, an offshore trust can include conventional estate planning strategies, including a credit shelter trust (the $650,000 exempt transfer amount), tax-exempt gifts ($10,000 per year per recipient), QTIP benefits (the unlimited tax-free transfers that may go to a surviving spouse), family limited partnerships, and other estate planning advantages obtainable only through the use of an offshore trust. For a family with substantial assets, Coxon says, the greatest advantage of an offshore trust is that after you die, the trust is never again subject to estate tax.

This may sound complex, and as attorney Kirk emphasizes, it is important that the process is handled correctly to avoid pitfalls. However, offshore trust information packages are available to simplify the procedure and make it more convenient and economical. The advantages of an offshore trust are no longer limited to the very rich, and may be practical for investors who want to place as little as $50,000 in this type of trust. Such trusts usually take care of themselves, and require little or nothing in the way of ongoing management from grantor, protector, or beneficiary.

Again, if you are contemplating any offshore arrangement, consult with advisers who have proven expertise in this area. Tax laws, IRS regulations, and important court decisions affect and often change the laws governing this type of trust. Setting up the trust can be complex, and may require additional knowledge in the fields of international investments, limited partnerships, limited-liability companies, and other highly specialized fields. Some reputable organizations that assist clients interested in this type of trust are listed in the Appendix.

A Word of Caution About Trusts

The Internal Revenue Service recently announced an effort to identify "abusive" trusts, defined as those that are promoted by unscrupulous investment advisers who describe them as devices for completely escaping income and estate taxes. Anything that makes such grandiose claims should raise a red flag, because such claims are almost certainly fraudulent.

Referred to by some legitimate investment advisers as "wishful trusts," these fraudulent types are presented under different guises. One common scam, known as a "family charitable trust," is supposedly exempt from income tax. The investor is set up as trustee of his own trust account and when he needs cash, the "charitable" trust makes a gift, supposedly tax-free, to the investor or to another family member.

According to reports by Passport Financial, a highly respected company with substantial expertise in legitimate estate planning and tax-shelter devices, such trust scams depend upon an investor's willingness to believe what he wants to believe. A mere legal structure cannot make all tax liabilities evaporate, and those who believe this is possible are ripe for exploitation by unscrupulous advisers. The eventual result for such a wishful investor can often be a painful bill for back taxes, including penalties and interest. Realistic tax planning and legitimate trust programs aim to turn big tax bills into small ones by whittling away at the problem, not by pretending to slay it with a single chop from a magic ax.

Deferring taxable income, replacing income-earning investments with appreciating investments, avoiding premature capital gains, and gradually shifting wealth out of your taxable estate may seem like slow work compared with a "wishful" trust program. But it gets the job done, and it keeps your tax life noncontroversial.

Groups such as Passport often offer trust packages to be used by clients along with the assistance of their attorneys and/or accountants, as well as offer publications, consulting services, or other forms of assistance. You should thoroughly check the background and reputation of any adviser you work with in setting up any type of tax-minimizing trust.

UNMARRIED COUPLES

Most of the same estate planning devices available to married couples may also be used by unmarried domestic partners, with a few important exceptions: first, those forms of joint marital ownership or inheritance rights that are imposed by state law, such as community property, spousal share, and intestate inheritance; second, the marital estate tax exemption; and third, bypass trusts that rely upon this exemption. However, with careful planning, such couples can take other steps to achieve most of the same goals.

Ruth B. Cohen, an attorney in Albuquerque, New Mexico, assists many lesbians, gays, and other nontraditional couples in preparing the documents necessary to meet their goals in estate planning and other areas. "Primarily, I make sure people have the necessary wills or living trusts, along with living wills, power of attorney, co-parenting agreements, and relationship agreements," she explains.

Cohen frequently presents seminars on legal protection for lesbians, gays, and their families, in which she covers a number of estate planning issues, including the importance of powers of attorney for nontraditional couples to deal with health-care issues, financial decisions and transactions, child-related responsibilities, and the difference between durable and nondurable documents. Cohen also provides general information on wills and living trusts, including issues of special concern to nontraditional couples.

"It's crucial for nontraditional couples to state their wishes in writing," she advises. "Durable powers of attorney for health care are especially important. In addition to the decision-making authority everyone should address, there are issues that come up for lesbians and gays, especially, because health-care providers may not recognize them as a couple." Cohen points out that a domestic partner may be denied information about her companion's condition or even the right to visit, unless there is a document addressing the issue. "Often, the health-care staff won't share information with someone who has not been recognized as a family member. If you want your partner to be able to do all the things a spouse could do without a piece of paper, this must be spelled out in your power of attorney."

Financial matters should also be considered carefully, she adds. "Because you are in a relationship that is not defined by law in the way a traditional marriage relationship is, you need different documents. And it is essential to put things in writing before you find yourself in the middle of a traumatic situation."

Lesbians and gays who are not presently in a domestic relationship, or those who do not wish to designate their partner as the person responsible for health-care decisions should also be sure to make a durable power of attorney that specifies who is to have this authority. "There may be a particular relative or friend you want to handle these decisions, and it's important that your health-care providers have this information in writing," Cohen advises.

Property issues must also be given special attention for nontraditional couples. If an unmarried couple wishes to share ownership of specific property, for estate planning or other purposes, the agreement must be in writing. Beneficiary designations in life insurance and retirement plans are also crucial, because in most cases, unless a specific beneficiary is named, the proceeds go to a blood relative designated by the plan. People have been surprised and disappointed to learn that a bequest in their will or living trust cannot override the requirement that a beneficiary be designated on the policy or account document.

Joint tenancy, tenancy in common, or other property sharing agreements may be in the form of deeds, partnership agreements, or other documents signed by both parties. The partners in such agreements are free to dispose of only their share of jointly held property, unless the contract or partnership agreement provides otherwise. Property held by unmarried couples in joint tenancy automatically goes to the survivor when one of them dies.

Cohen frequently assists her clients in placing property, such as real estate, into individually structured ownership agreements that are right for them. "For those who do not wish to own property in joint tenancy, I draft agreements that spell out each partner's equitable share," she explains. "And in any type of agreement I prepare for nontraditional couples, I urge them to include a clause that provides that they will try mediation before litigation if a dispute arises."

Litigation, while always unpleasant, can be especially problematic for gays and lesbians. "I try to help my clients avoid litigation for two reasons," she explains. "First, since their relationship is not legally defined, any court action will be more complex, drawn out, and frustrating. Second, there is still a fair amount of homophobia in the courts, although judges are getting better about treating such couples fairly. If possible, it's much better to settle a dispute through mediation."

One advantage of living trusts, as opposed to wills, is that it may be more difficult to contest a trust than a will, Cohen says. "A living trust is drafted for use during your lifetime, as well as distributing property after death, so people are less likely to claim that you were pressured in some way," she explains. "Another advantage that may be important to those in nontraditional relationships is confidentiality. Of course, the disadvantage is that setting up a trust costs more than preparing a will."

Several issues in estate planning may be significant for unmarried couples, she notes. "Nontraditional couples face special parenting issues both during their lifetime, and if one or both parents die while they are raising a child who is still a minor at the time of death. If you are raising a child with your partner, it's important to address guardianship issues in your will. I often include the clause to cover children not yet born if one partner is pregnant, for example, to insure that custody issues are decided and stated in writing in the event that the biological parent dies or becomes disabled during the pregnancy or during childbirth."

Cohen also pays special attention to the law regarding the steps that must be taken to exclude blood relatives. "Under New Mexico case law, to effectively exclude a blood relative, you must state who you are excluding and why, and list the names of those excluded." Cohen works with her clients to draft a clause in their wills that explains the decision was made consciously. Where a domestic partner is the beneficiary, the clause emphasizes that the testator has had a long-term emotional and financial relationship with that person.

For those with estates large enough to subject them to estate taxation, Cohen notes, carefully structured inter vivos gifts can often help take the place of the tax advantages available to married couples. "Talk to a financial planner or attorney who is well-versed in this aspect of estate planning if this is a concern," she advises.

Good books that detail and provide sample property-sharing agreements for married couples are available (see Appendix). The laws governing property rights between unmarried couples apply equally to gay, lesbian, or heterosexual couples. In many areas, gay and lesbian organizations provide workshops for couples who wish to learn about and rearrange their property rights. Such presentations can also be valuable for unmarried heterosexual couples.

ANIMALS

Surprisingly, providing for the care of a pet can be one of the trickiest bits of business in the estate-planning process. The law is picky about what sorts of creature comfort provisions it will and will not enforce, and law books are full of stories about estates that were unsuccessfully willed to a pet. The general rule is that you can't will money or property to an animal, only to humans or institutions. Likewise, in most states, an animal cannot be the beneficiary of a trust. However, this law is changing. California and Tennessee allow people to leave money or property to an animal, and at least eight states now allow trust funds to be created for the *care of* animals.

In any jurisdiction, there are ways to effectively provide for a creature's care. You may enter into a contract with the person who will receive the animal after you die or become incapacitated, and then leave that individual money in your will to pay for the pet's care. The better technique is generally to set up a trust that provides to a person who is named as the beneficiary of the trust a sum of money for the animal's care. Then the animal is passed to this person by a will.

Anyone you designate to care for pets or livestock should be willing, and fully capable, of doing so. Do not forget to consider special circumstances or legal requirements if you have large, exotic, or licensed animals. For example, falconers who own birds of prey are subject to stringent state and federal licensing regulations. Hawks and falcons may be legally held only by someone with the right license and permit, and the number of birds each falconer may have at a given time is limited. All falconers know this, because licensing requirements include a written test that covers these laws, but people may not think about such things in the context of estate planning. For other exotic animals, such as ferrets, state laws vary.

People sometimes assume that if they bequeath an animal to a zoo or similar facility, this will guarantee its care, but even zoos and educational institutions are subject to both practical and legal limits on the types and numbers of animals they may keep. You must thoroughly discuss all of the applicable considerations with anyone to whom you plan to leave a living creature, and make sure that they are both willing and able to assume responsibility for its care.

PARENTS OF MINOR CHILDREN

If you have children younger than eighteen (or in some states, twenty-one), you must take special steps to ensure that they are cared for if you die before they become adults. First, and often foremost, you and your spouse should choose a person to be named as guardian to supervise your child and his property during his minority if you and your spouse both die.

In most cases, the same person who becomes a child's legal guardian also takes care of property the parents left to the child. In other cases, especially when the parents owned substantial assets that now belong to the child, a different person is named as a "property guardian," or if a special trust is established, as trustee. (Some common trusts for children were discussed in the previous chapter.) In such a case, it is important to distinguish between the different forms of guardianship.

Those with complex assets may wish to consider naming a different person to manage money that would be left for the child's benefit, as trustee of a property control trust or as property guardian. Usually, the same person is chosen to fill both roles, but those with complex investments, for example, may wish to name someone with expertise in this area to handle this property.

Legal or Custodial Guardianship

Estate planning attorneys stress that everyone with minor children should have a will to name a guardian for their children, regardless of the other tools they use to plan their estate. The will can be a simple, two-page document for this purpose alone. If parents do not choose someone to raise their children if they die, there is no guarantee who may be appointed by the court. Some horrible choices have been made when the parents did not have a will.

While many people name a family member to act as custodial guardian for their children, and there is a legal presumption in some state statutes favoring family members, as a general rule you are free to choose any competent adult.

More and more couples today are choosing close friends to fill this role. For example, Jim and Paula decided to make wills after the birth of their son. Like many people, they first considered their siblings. Paula had a sister and a brother, but her sister, although a good mother to her own daughter, lived in a distant state, and her own marriage was both financially and emotionally troubled. Paula's brother lived nearby, but while she felt close to him, she disliked his wife, whom she believed had been a terrible mother to their son. As for Jim, he had three younger sisters who lived near the family, and all got along fairly well. But both Jim and Paula felt that his sisters tended to be competitive, materialistic, and shallow, and only one was married with a child of her own. So they looked to their best friends as potential candidates.

Paula's best friend was married, and lived in a distant but highly desirable community. However, she and her husband had recently decided that they were not cut out to be parents and did not plan to have a family of their own. Therefore, they were ruled out. Jim's best friend and his wife, a woman some years his senior who had already successfully raised a son, were finally chosen as the best candidates. Both had indicated that they would like more children, and were kind, stable, responsible people who lived nearby and would enable Jim and Paula's son to maintain contact with his grandparents and other family members. When Jim and Paula approached the couple, they said they would be honored to be the boy's guardian if anything happened to his parents.

The latter factor is one of the most important in choosing someone to act as guardian. While it may be awkward, it is essential to discuss the matter with the person or couple you name, and make sure they are willing to accept the responsibility should a tragedy occur.

Sometimes people who are divorced would prefer that someone other than their former spouse raise the child if they die. But unless the other parent has been declared unfit by a court, in most cases, custody of the child goes to the living natural parent.

However, if you have strong feelings about this issue, you may designate a different preferred guardian, and the court will consider what is in the best interest of the child. If there has been no official declaration that the other parent is unfit, but you have evidence such as proof of abuse or neglect that suggests this would be the case, inform your lawyer of this. She should have copy of police reports, court orders granting you sole custody, or other evidence.

Asset Management and Property Guardians

If your child would inherit substantial assets upon the death of you and your spouse, you may want to consider alternatives for management of the child's property, such as a specific form of property control trust, or a transfer under the Uniform Transfers to Minors Act, adopted by many states. These devices are discussed in chapter 6.

While you still need a will to nominate a legal guardian, subject to the court's approval, a trust can give you a measure of control over who will manage the assets you wish to leave to your children, as well as greater power to say how the assets should be used. An appropriate trust may be created as a part of your will or living trust, or as a separate agreement.

When substantial assets are left to minor children in the absence of such a trust, the court is required by law to establish a guardianship for those assets. As a part of this process, it names a guardian to use the money for the benefit of the children. The guardian must go back to court every year to account for the money spent for the children. This means for the guardian the burden of meticulous accounting and reporting, as well as legal fees and related costs. Also, when each child reaches majority, the remaining funds must be handed over, regardless of his ability to manage the money. Your wishes that the money be spent for certain purposes, such as a college education, may be disregarded if the child does not choose to follow them.

Setting up some type of property control trust allows you to decide how, when, and for what purposes your children will receive their money if you die while they are minors. This also enables you to appoint successor trustees, such as your chosen legal guardian for the children, to manage and distribute the money for the children's benefit. This type of arrangement avoids the headaches and expense of yearly reporting and accounting to the court, as well as the accompanying fees. With this type of trust, you may also specify that the money will not go to the children until they reach a set age, which can extend beyond their majority, or, for example, after they have earned a college degree. Each trust can be drafted to suit your own family's goals and preferences.

Trusts created for children are usually structured so that the principal will be distributed to the child at some specific time. This is called the "ultimate distribution," and may be managed in a variety of ways. Some trusts provide that all of the remaining funds will go to the person as soon as he reaches a set age or some particular event takes place, such as when the person marries or earns a college degree. Others provide for incremental distribution, for example, one-third of the funds at the beneficiary's twenty-fifth, thirtieth, and thirty-fifth birthdays. Some leave the decision up to the trustee, who distributes the property when he feels that the beneficiary needs or deserves it, for example, when the beneficiary decides to buy a home.

TRUSTS FOR THOSE WITH SPECIAL NEEDS

If you wish to plan for the care of someone with special needs, such as a disabled person, be sure the trust is drawn up by someone with expertise in this area. People with disabilities are often eligible for government assistance through Social Security, educational grants, and other beneficial programs. Trusts for such people must meet specific requirements if the beneficiary is to remain eligible for these benefits, and should always be set up by someone with training in this area.

INTELLECTUAL PROPERTY AND OTHER CONTINUING INCOME TO THE ESTATE

The creative works of artists, writers, actors, inventors, and others whose efforts bring income long after the work is completed need special care and attention in the estate planning process. A popular book, a patented scientific process, or a musical composition may continue to provide income for the creator's beneficiaries for decades via royalties, residuals, or contractual licensing agreements—but only if these important property interests are handled *carefully* in the estate plan.

The transfer of intellectual property rights after the creator's death requires special knowledge of copyright, trademark, patent, and other specific laws that govern such rights. Anyone with an ownership interest in intellectual property should take special care to ensure that these rights are addressed, even if they do not appear to be especially valuable at the time. Your heirs could miss out on the opportunity for important, valuable property rights if they are not meticulously protected—or, they could enjoy great benefits if you take some relatively simple steps to guard this property.

For example, F. Scott Fitzgerald, now considered to be one of the greatest authors of American literature, enjoyed early popular success, and then faded into relative obscurity. When he died in 1940, most of his works were out of print. Despite his difficulties, however, Fitzgerald had always believed in the value of his work and took the necessary steps to protect his rights in it. Therefore, as his writing regained acclaim and began to produce substantial royalties, Fitzgerald's decedents have continued to benefit from the fruits of his labors.

Achieving full protection of intellectual property rights and the profits from them can be a complex matter, even for those who try hard to do so, especially when family disputes, or other odd circumstances, complicate the situation. For example, author Jack Kerouac, one of the leading voices of the "beat" generation, died in 1969. At the time, his estate was divided between his wife and mother. Yet, the final resolution of Kerouac's estate, including substantial royalties along with control and protection of these intangible assets, remains in limbo some thirty years after his death.

Kerouac's daughter Jan, herself a published writer, made a detailed will appointing a special "literary executor," in addition to the regular executor, to specifically oversee the literary property rights belonging to both her and her father. But when Jan Kerouac died in New Mexico in 1996, she was still involved in litigation over her father's literary properties as passed through her grandmother's estate, which was pending in a Florida court. In probating Jan Kerouac's estate, the New Mexico court was called upon to interpret the scope of the literary executor's authority, a matter the courts of that state had not previously considered. As a result, the ultimate fate of several estates and unique property rights remains in litigation in two different states.

Jan Kerouac likely did the best she could to try to protect these rights, but it is often difficult to predict what complications may arise, especially when intellectual property rights are involved. Ironically, when someone tries to go the extra mile to protect such assets, it may have the opposite effect. In the Kerouac cases, both the Florida and New Mexico court opinions reveal apparent confusion over the role and responsibility of a literary executor. As a result, it appears unlikely that the ultimate result will be what Jan Kerouac intended to achieve through her will.

Sometimes the testator's wishes are simply beyond the scope of what the law can provide in the face of conflicting interests. For example, Ernest Hemingway often stated adamantly during his lifetime that he did not wish for any of his private correspondence or unfinished works to be published after his death. Although Hemingway took various steps to try to see that his wishes in this regard would be respected, including a specific letter to his executor, this type of control is difficult to maintain indefinitely, especially when both the publishing and academic communities have such a strong interest in such materials. As a result, since Hemingway's death in 1961, the majority of these items have now been published in some form. Members of the Hemingway family and Hemingway scholars have managed through control of the context and editing of these materials to maintain some balance between the late writer's expressed wishes and the desire of so many others for access to this work.

Ideally, anyone who owns significant intellectual property rights would be well advised to employ the services of a top-notch estate planning attorney, as well as a lawyer with expertise in both the law and business aspects of the particular media involved—whether it be art, science, literature, or another field. Intellectual property interests and rights may be transferred to your beneficiaries through a will or living trust in the same manner as tangible personal property. Be aware that you may not be able to anticipate or control all the contingencies that may arise years down the road. Do the best you can to preserve and protect your creations, and then accept the fact that none of us will be able to control forever what happens to the fruits of our labors after our demise.

WHEN, WHY, AND HOW TO REVIEW AND CHANGE YOUR ESTATE PLAN

For most people, estate planning is not a onetime event but a process that requires periodic updating and review. As the story in the introduction illustrates, it is absolutely essential that you and your advisers give all the documents a final once-over after they are drafted, to be sure that there are no mistakes or omissions. Thereafter, wills and other documents must be reviewed and, if necessary, updated whenever there are significant changes in your life or in the lives of others named in the document. Major life events that make a review of your plan essential include retirement, divorce, birth, or adoption of a child, and the death of a spouse or beneficiary.

However, lesser transformations can also signal a need to look at your existing plan to consider whether revisions may be necessary. If you have become more prosperous since you initially made your estate plan, have taken over the care of an elderly parent, moved to another state, bought or sold real estate or a business, or, if many years have passed since you reviewed your plan, it may be time to examine your arrangements.

Anytime you change one part of your estate plan, consider how this may affect the overall scheme. "If you change one component of your estate plan, it is important to review everything else that will be affected by that change," says attorney Tom Horne, who advises clients to be especially careful when incorporating something such as an older trust into a new will. "Mistakes occur in documents all the time," he says. "Be sure everything is correct, complete, and that you understand how it all works together."

Even if you have experienced no major changes, it is wise to occasionally review your estate plan. Many people look over their estate documents every year when they prepare their tax returns, or in conjunction with some special date or event, such as New Year's Day or on their birthday. At a minimum, it is essential to review the documents anytime there is a substantial change in your life involving your assets, income, family, or anytime your financial picture has changed.

Many attorneys also advise clients to be aware of changes in the law, especially tax laws, that may affect their estate plan. Some accountants and attorneys who specialize in tax planning provide newsletters informing their clients of significant changes. If yours do not, you may want to check with an accountant each year when you do your annual taxes to see if any legal changes have occurred that may affect your estate plan.

Divorce and Estate Planning

Divorce can have innumerable consequences that impact your estate plan. Property that was held as community or marital property changes its character, debts are reapportioned, assets change hands and sometimes value, parenting issues must be addressed, and life insurance and retirement needs change.

State laws vary about how a divorce affects an estate plan. In New Mexico, for example, the law states that when a person is divorced, a spouse named in the will is automatically presumed to be out. But the divorce still affects the estate plan, and this provision is not included in the law of all states.

You should, if possible, review your estate plan and begin making changes while you are involved in the divorce process rather than waiting for the divorce to be final. If one spouse dies before the divorce is final, this can complicate settlement of the estate considerably and lead to unnecessary difficulty, cost, and emotional pain for family members and other beneficiaries.

Some of the specific concerns that should be addressed before or during the divorce will probably become obvious, such as changing your will or living trust, changing beneficiary designations on life insurance and retirement policies, and transferring title to assets. Sometimes a divorce decree specifies that a noncustodial parent will continue to name a minor child as beneficiary on a life insurance policy, for example. In other cases, people outline a detailed division of property and debts in a divorce decree but do not follow up on the paperwork required to make these changes effective, such as executing quitclaim or other deeds to transfer real estate from joint ownership to one person, or working with creditors to close and reopen a credit-card account in one partner's name alone. If these follow-up duties are not completed, it can wreak havoc on both current personal business and an estate plan.

Relocation

If you move to another state, you may be subject to different laws, which can have a major impact on your estate plan. For example, probate laws, laws of intestate succession, and, especially, community-property or marital-property laws all may operate to effectively change the plan you have crafted. If you have any concern that these laws may affect your plan, particularly in community-property states, discuss this with an attorney familiar with the laws of the state where you are now domiciled.

Remarriage, and Blended or Stepfamilies

Divorced or widowed parents who remarry often face special challenges when trying to devise a fair, comprehensive estate plan that provides for all their loved ones. This may require a change in an existing will or trust, the purchase of additional life insurance, and in many cases, the establishment of some type of marital trust.

As discussed in the last chapter, marital trusts or other tools may be used to give your spouse a life estate in certain property, such as the family home and its furnishings, and then pass these assets to your children or other beneficiaries when she dies. This type of trust can also be used to manage money, stocks, or other assets. Restrictions are usually placed on the assets so that they will be preserved, for example, by providing that your spouse receives the interest from an account during her lifetime. Then the principal passes to your children. It may be tricky to structure this type of arrangement so that everyone you want to protect receives adequate, accessible benefits, but with a little creative planning and competent help, as in most estate-planning challenges, your goals can usually be achieved.

APPENDIX

RESOURCES AND SUGGESTED READINGS

"AARP Perspectives." *Modern Maturity,* July–August 1998, p. 88.

ABA Section of Real Property, Probate and Trust Law. *Business Succession Planning and Beyond: A Multidisciplinary Approach to Representing the Family-Owned Business.* Chicago: ABA Services. 1998.

American Bar Association. *The American Bar Association Guide to Wills and Estates.* New York: Random House/Times Books, 1995.

Appel, Jens C. and F. Bruce Gentry. *The Complete Probate Kit.* New York: John Wiley & Sons, 1991.
(Comment: This provides good information and general guidelines for those serving as personal representatives or executors.)

Carver, Randy. "Living Trusts: Fact and Fiction." http:\\www.bullmkt.com\living.html.

Clifford, Denis and Cora Jordon. *Plan Your Estate: Absolutely Everything You Need to Know to Protect your Loved Ones.* 4th ed. Berkeley: Nolo Press, 1998.

Coxon, Terry. *Keep What You Earn.* New York: Times Books/Random House, 1996.

——— "Powerful Protection with an Offshore Trust." *Personal Investing News,* fall 1998, p. 10.

Dacey, Norman F. *How to Avoid Probate!,* New York: Collier Books, 1990. (Comment: Dacey's classic volume is a good source of information on the various types of trusts that can be established as part of an estate plan. However, beware his insistence that you can do it all yourself—the tear-out forms he provides may or may not be right for your individual circumstances and particular jurisdiction.)

Esperti, Robert A. and Renno L. Peterson. *The Living Trust Revolution.* New York: Viking Penguin, 1992.

Hughes, Theodore E. and David Klein. *A Family Guide to Estate Planning, Funeral Arrangements, and Settling an Estate After Death.* New York: Charles Scribner's Sons, 1983.

Knox, Lucinda Pagge and Michael Knox. *Last Wishes: A Handbook to Guide Your Survivors.* Berkeley: Ulysses Press, 1995.

Manning, Jerome A. *Estate Planning: How to Preserve Your Estate for Your Loved Ones.* New York: Practicing Law Institute, 1992.

Martindale-Hubble Law Digest
(Comment: Available in most public libraries and updated yearly, this volume contains concise summaries of the statutory law of each state, listed by topic. [See "Estates and Trusts."] It can provide a basic overview of your state's probate and related laws, and guide you to the specific statutes.)

Orman, Suze. *The 9 Steps to Financial Freedom.* New York: Crown Publishers, Inc., 1997.

"Passport Financial Offshore Trust Alert." Austin: Passport Financial, Inc., 1997.

Rudd, Merri. *Life Planning in New Mexico.* Albuquerque: Abogada Press, 1992.

Schenkman, Martin. *Estate Planning After the 1997 Tax Act.* New York: John Wiley & Sons, 1998.

Strauss, Stephen D. *Ask A Lawyer: Wills and Trusts.* New York: W.W. Norton & Co., 1998.

Szabo, Joan. "Tax Talk: Estate of Affairs." *Entrepreneur*, May 1998, p. 71.

Welch, Mark J. "Your Will or Trust is Not A Complete Estate Plan." *Mark Welch's Legal Advisory Newsletter*, summer 1994.

INTERNET WEB SITES

As of early 1999, several excellent Web sites are found at the following locations:

American Academy of Estate Planning Attorneys
http://www.aaepa.com

American Bar Association
http://www.abanet.org/

Cornell University Law School
http://www.law.cornell.edu/topics/estate_planning.html

Findlaw
http://www.findlaw.com/oitopics/31probate/index.html

National Network of Estate Planning Attorneys
http://www.netplanning.com/

Martindale-Hubbell
http://www.martindale.com/
This site, maintained by the largest publisher of law digests and directories, provides information on how to reach most attorneys, both in the United States and internationally.

National Network of Estate Planning Attorneys
www.netplanning.com/
This organization is dedicated to the enhancement of estate planning practice for both attorneys and clients. It provides public information, seminars for professionals, and maintains an on-line member list.

Nolo.com Self-Help law center
http://www.1040.174.208.58/ChunkEP/EP.index.html
Nolo, a publisher of self-help law books, provides a good overview of estate planning topics and general information, along with jokes, games, and lawyer humor.

U.S. Estate Planning and Trust Attorneys
http://www.ca-probate.com/attylist.htm
This site lists estate attorneys with Web sites, indexed by state, and provides links to these and other sites with estate planning information.

Celebrity Wills
http://www.ca-probate.com/wills.htm
More fascinating than informative, this site links to wills of many famous and otherwise interesting people, including Ben Franklin, Marilyn Monroe, Babe Ruth, and, of course, Elvis Presley.

Attorney Mark J. Welch
http://www.ca-probate.com/
This California estate-planning lawyer maintains an extensive web site with links to articles and information on various estate planning topics.

ORGANIZATIONS

Lawyers and Other Legal Groups

American Bar Association
Section on Real Property, Probate, and Trust Law
750 North Lakeshore Drive
Chicago, IL 60611
1-800-621-6159
(312) 988-5000
Web site: http://www.abanet.org/
E-mail: info@abanet.org/
The ABA publishes various materials, provides consumer and professional education, information, and referrals.

American College of Estate and Trust Counsel
3415 South Sepulveda Boulevard, Suite 330
Los Angeles, CA 90034
(310) 398-1888
Web site: www.actec.org/
E-mail: info@acetc.org
This professional association of U.S. lawyers who are skilled and experienced in the preparation of wills, trusts, and other estate-planning issues; and have been nominated and elected by fellows of the college. Produces publications and makes referrals to members for consumers. Write for a list of members in your area.

American Academy of Estate Planning Attorneys
4250 Executive Square, Suite 900
La Jolla, CA 92037
1-800-846-1555
E-mail: information@aaepa.com
This organization maintains an excellent Internet Web site, provides general information, news about estate planning issues, publications, referrals to members, including an on-line listing, one on one technical assistance to its members on estate planning issues as well as formal training on written updates and estate planning documents.

Financial Planning Groups

Certified Financial Planner Board of Standards
1700 Broadway, No. 2100
Denver, CO 80290
(303) 830-7500
Web site: http://www.cfp.board.org
E-mail: Mail@cfp.board.org
Publishes consumer guides, booklets, and brochures.

Institute of Certified Financial Planners
3801 East Florida Avenue, Suite 708
Denver, CO 80201-2500
1-800-322-4237
(303) 759-4900
Seeks to maintain high professional standards in financial planning, licenses Certified Financial Planners; conducts seminars, maintains a referral service.

International Association for Financial Planning
5775 Glenridge Drive NE, Suite B-300
Atlanta, GA 30328-5364
(404) 845-0011
Provides names of financial planners and analysts who have met rigorous requirements for membership.

Registered Financial Planners Institute
2001 Cooper Foster Park Road
Amherst, OH 44001
(216) 282-7176
E-mail: rfp@rfpi.com
Organization of registered financial planners awards RFP designation to qualified members, promotes high standards in financial planning, maintains a referral service, and a speakers bureau.

The following firms offer information and assistance on offshore investments and/or foreign corporations:

Passport Financial, Inc.
207 Jefferson Square
Austin, TX 78731
1-800-531-5142
www.PassportTrust.com

Private Investments Limited
112 West San Francisco Street, Suite 303
Santa Fe, NM 87501
1-800-844-4888

Robert B. Martin, Jr.
Attorney at Law
350 West Colorado Boulevard, Suite 320
Pasadena, CA 91105
(818) 793-8500

Funeral Planning and Related Services

Cemetery Consumer Service Council
P.O. Box 3574
Washington, DC 20007
(703) 379-6426
Information about plot purchase, other cemetery-related goods and services.

Cremation Association of North America
401 North Michigan Avenue
Chicago, IL 60611
(312) 644-6610
Offers pamphlets on cremation.

Funeral and Memorial Societies of America
6900 Lost Lake Road
Egg Harbor, WI 54209
1-800-458-5563
(414) 868-3136
Offers information about nonprofit memorial societies, simpler and more affordable funerals, and wholesale caskets. May charge small fee or donation for materials.

Funeral Service Consumer Assistance Program
2250 East Devon Avenue, Suite 250
Des Plaines, IL 60018
1-800-662-7666
This nonprofit organization provides consumer information on death, grief, preplanned funeral services. Publishes pamphlets.

Jewish Funeral Directors of America
399 East 72nd Street, Suite 3F
New York, NY 10021
(212) 628-3465
Provides grief counseling and referrals to local counseling services, funeral preplanning, and various publications.

National Funeral Directors Association
11121 West Oklahoma Avenue
Milwaukee, WI 53227
(414) 541-2500
Offers free pamphlets on funeral services.

Insurance Quotes

Insurance Quote Services
1-800-972-1104
http://www.iquote.com

Master Quote
1-800-337-5433
http://www.masterquote.com

Quote Smith
1-800-431-1147
http://www.quotesmith.com

Termquote
1-800-444-8376
http://www.rcinet.com/~termquote

Liferates of America
1-800-457-2837

Select Quote
1-800-343-1985

Wholesale Insurance Network
1-800-808-5810

Other Organizations

Internal Revenue Service
Information: 1-800-829-1040
Forms: 1-800-829-3676
Web site: www.irs.ustreas.gov/prod/cover.html

Medicare Hotline: 1-800-638-6833

Social Security Administration: 1-800-772-1213

Veterans Administration: 1-800-827-8019

Winthrop Mutual Fund: Offers a family document checklist that may be ordered by calling 1-800-225-8011

American Association of Retired Persons (AARP)
601 E Street NW
Washington, DC 20049-0001
(202) 434-2277
Offers many publications.

Elisabeth Kübler-Ross Center
South Route 616
Headwaters, VA 24442
(703) 396-3441

Viatical Association of America
1200 19th Street NW, Suite 300
Washington, DC 20036-2422
1-800-842-9811
(202) 429-5129
Web site: http://www.viatical.org/viatical
This organization seeks to inform the public, legislators, and officials about viatical settlements, in which the terminally ill may convert existing life insurance into cash to meet critical financial needs.

National Association of Professional Organizers
1033 La Posada Drive, Suite 220
Austin, TX 78752-3880
(512) 454-8626
Members are professional organizers who provide home and business organization services.

Choice in Dying, Inc.
200 Varick Street, 10th Floor
New York, NY 10014-4810
1-800-989-9455
This nonprofit organization advocates patients' rights to make their own decision about treatment and to receive dignified, compassionate care at the end of their lives. It provides directive forms for each state.

The Living Bank
P.O. Box 6725
Houston, TX 77265
1-800-528-2971
Provides forms to be executed by those wishing to be organ and tissue donors.

Lambda Legal Defense and Education Fund
120 Wall Street, Suite 1500
New York, NY 10005-3904
(212) 809-8585
Web site: http://www.lambdalegal.org
This organization promotes the civil rights of gays and lesbians, and provides information on various legal concerns.

INDEX